the friendship project

"In an age that values social networks over face-to-face relationships, Michele Faehnle and Emily Jaminet make a compelling case for the lost art of spiritual friendship. They draw from a rich vein of personal experience and the lives of the saints to prove that the old proverb is still true: to have a friend, you must be a friend. Read this book to find out how."

Colleen Carroll Campbell
Author of *My Sisters the Saints*

"We live in a technology-driven world where people are instantly connected, yet in our own personal lives, we often feel isolated and alone. Each of us is 'hard-wired' to love and to be loved—to live in communion. *The Friendship Project* is an inspiring and uplifting answer to how we can be internally connected and equipped to form lasting friendships—first with God and second with others. It underscores the truth that happiness lies in living a virtuous life."

Sr. John Dominic, O.P.
Developer of *Disciple of Christ, Education in Virtue*

"The Bible says that 'a faithful friend is a sturdy shelter and he that has found one has found a treasure.' The same goes for finding this book! We are all a work in progress, and while finding virtuous friendships can be difficult, they are *vital* in life. *The Friendship Project* shows us just how to find and invest in these intentional and virtuous friendships. Thank you, Michele and Emily, for writing such a treasure!"

Sarah Swafford
Speaker and author of
Emotional Virtue: A Guide to Drama-Free Relationships

"This book is truly a gift from God. A very practical guide to help women develop and enhance great Christian friendships."

Fr. Larry Richards
Pastor, Relevant Radio host, and founder of
The Reason for our Hope Foundation

the friendship project

The *Catholic Woman's* Guide to Making and Keeping Fabulous, Faith-Filled *Friends*

MICHELE FAEHNLE
EMILY JAMINET

Foreword by Fr. Larry Richards

AVE MARIA PRESS AVE Notre Dame, Indiana

© 2017 by Michele Faehnle and Emily Jaminet

Founded in 1865, Ave Maria Press is a ministry of the United States Province of Holy Cross.

www.avemariapress.com

Paperback: ISBN-13 978-1-59471-761-1

E-book: ISBN-13 978-1-59471-762-8

Cover images ©Ivona Staszewski, available on her shop. evonagallery.com and www.etsy.com/shop/Evonagallery.

Cover design by Kristen Hornyak Bonelli and Katherine Robinson.

Text design by Katherine Robinson.

Printed and bound in the United States of America.

Library of Congress Cataloging-in-Publication Data is available.

To all of our friends,

thank you

for being part of our lives!

Pleasant speech multiplies friends,
    and gracious lips, friendly greetings.
Let those who are friendly to you be many,
    but one in a thousand your confidant.
When you gain friends, gain them through testing,
    and do not be quick to trust them.
For there are friends when it suits them,
    but they will not be around in time of trouble.
Another is a friend who turns into an enemy,
    and tells of the quarrel to your disgrace.
Others are friends, table companions,
    but they cannot be found in time of affliction.
When things go well, they are your other self,
    and lord it over your servants.
If disaster comes upon you, they turn against you
    and hide themselves.
Stay away from your enemies,
    and be on guard with your friends.
Faithful friends are a sturdy shelter;
    whoever finds one finds a treasure.
Faithful friends are beyond price,
    no amount can balance their worth.
Faithful friends are life-saving medicine;
    those who fear God will find them.
Those who fear the Lord enjoy stable friendship,
    for as they are, so will their neighbors be.

—Sirach 6:5–17

Contents

Foreword

I am sure some of you are laughing that I am the one to write the foreword to this wonderful book on friendship between women, especially since I am best known for speaking at men's conferences and writing the book *Be a Man!* I, too, have to admit that when I was first asked to do the foreword for a book on women and friendship, I was a little intimidated. But when I read the book, I was struck by just how important a topic friendship is and that, no matter if we are women or men, God created us for friendship and anything that can make us better friends is a gift of God. This book is truly a gift from God, and it is a very practical guide to help women develop and enhance great Christian friendships.

The sacred scriptures also give examples of and advise on friendship.

From the beginning of the Bible, we hear God speak one of the most fundamental truths: it is not good to be alone (see Genesis 2:18). God created us to be with others. We are not meant to be alone; he created us from the beginning to need others. Now Genesis 2:18 is, of course, the case between a husband and a wife, but it is also the case with friendship. When we have true friends, they can lead us to be better and stronger and to be more loving.

The book of Sirach speaks about the importance of friendship in the famous verse, "Faithful friends are a sturdy shelter; whoever finds one finds a treasure" (6:14). A treasure indeed! When we have faithful friends, when we are faithful friends, this can become the shelter to weather all of life's storms. Friends make our struggles bearable, and they help us to share the burdens that all life brings. Those who have good friends have more treasure than gold or money can provide.

Though friendship is so important, it has become a rare priority in our world today. The Internet and social media give the false promise of intimacy and friendship, but in fact they only separate us and isolate people all the more. Instead of having real conversations with others, we text them or message them or comment briefly on their pictures. Friendship is so much more than "friending" someone on Facebook! Friendship demands time and work, and we need to break through all the artificial stuff and dedicate ourselves to being good friends and having good friends. That is what this book will help you to do.

I think that the core of all friendship is the time we invest in it. There is no way to be a true friend unless you dedicate time to it. The most lasting friendships are those that have shared time and memories. Think of your own friends from your past; the people you have spent so much time with are the people who have become part of the fabric of your life. If we want to have more fulfilling friendships in the future then we must decide we are going to give the time and commitment that true friendship demands.

Everything we have said about friendship needs to be said about our relationship with God. For a Christian, the most important friendship should be with Jesus Christ. A hymn reminds us, "What a friend we have in Jesus!" When we focus on what friendship is, we need to look at Jesus, who is the model of all humankind. Jesus shows us through his life and in his Passion, Death, and Resurrection that he truly is a friend to us always and invites each of us to the deep intimacy of friendship with him. He even explicitly calls us his friends when he says, "I have called you friends" (Jn 15:15). Jesus calls *us* his friends!

If I were to ask you to write down the names of all your friends, would Jesus even make it on the list? I remember when I was a young seminarian in college working in the Grand Canyon, there was a Protestant girl there who was part of our group, and she came walking in one day and said, "Do you know what Jesus did for me today?" I was taken aback by this and thought, *Oh yeah, like you know Jesus that way.* The reality was that she did! I remember thinking that this was the kind of relationship I wanted with Jesus. I spent more time talking to him in prayer every day, and I spent more time learning about him in sacred scripture, so I could know him better as a friend.

As with all other friendships in our lives, our friendship with Jesus takes time and commitment. It is a give and take and not just one-sided. The only way to have a true friend is to spend time with them. We do this with Jesus when we pray. Do you have committed daily time with Jesus as your divine friend? He longs for you to be with him, and he calls you to this intimacy. And as with all friendship, we need to spend time with him each day.

Whether it is friendship with Jesus or with others, friendship is a treasure, and this book will help you to discover and use this treasure. It is filled with very prac-tical suggestions on how to be a better friend. I would encourage you to take some of these suggestions and apply them to your relationship with Jesus. May this book help you to be a better friend to others and to Jesus!

Fr. Larry Richards
Pastor of St. Joseph Church / Bread of Life Community and
founder of The Reason for Our Hope Foundation
Erie, Pennsylvania

Acknowledgments

We owe volumes of gratitude to all of our friends who helped us with this manuscript.

Most importantly, we thank our families: husbands Matt Faehnle and John Jaminet, our best friends and confidants, for their continued support and children Jacob, Mary Kate, Juliana, and Leah Faehnle and Nathan, Ben, Josh, Catherine, Andrew, Mary, and Elizabeth Jaminet for putting up with dirty houses and leftovers for dinner as we write and travel.

We would like to thank all those on the Ave Maria Press team who helped us through this journey, especially Lisa Hendey, Amber Elder, Tom Grady, Karey Circosta, Jared Dees, Heather Glenn, Kristen Hornyak Bonelli, and Stephanie Sibal.

We also would like to give a very big thank you to Elizabeth Pardi, Michelle Biagi and Mary Mitchell for guidance in the editing process; Jody White for assistance with marketing; Ali Arend for being our personal web designer and Internet guru; and Tami Kaiser for producing our videos. We also want to thank our friends whom you will meet in the upcoming pages and who have allowed us to share their stories.

Finally, we are very grateful to our faith-sharing group and all of our fabulous, faith-filled friends who have given us the gift of their friendship.

Introduction

Encountering Friendship—Emily

One of the greatest gifts and blessings in my life has been my friendships. On my fortieth birthday, I was reminded of all the wonderful people God had placed in my life. I woke up that Saturday to find that my husband had arranged for me to spend a full day with my friends. It began with a much-needed manicure and pedicure with two of my favorite people in the world, my sister, Ginny, and sister-in-law, Chrissy, followed by lunch with my college roommates, and ended with a birthday party that evening, attended by friends from all stages of my life.

As I lay in bed that night pondering the celebration, it dawned on me how blessed I was to have had amazing friends throughout my life. They had been there in good times and bad, consistently supporting me on my journey to become the daughter of God that he created me to be. These incredible friends constantly remind me of their love and God's through the thick and thin of life. However, while I have come to appreciate the great blessing of my friends, I know that not everyone has had relationships that have lasted a lifetime—or even fully values their friendships.

Throughout my enjoyment of that beautiful day of friendship, a conversation I had overheard earlier while getting my nails done haunted me. The girl next to me leaned over and declared, "I was the first person in the salon to use this particular shade of black." She proceeded to tell me all about her life, which consisted of work, her fiancée, her dog, and her favorite activity:

getting her nails done by her "friend," the nail technician. Every Saturday morning she would arrive at the
salon and tell the nail technician about her week. As
she talked, the technician would listen and work on
her nails. When her nails were done, she paid and said,
"See you next week."

It was obvious to me that the two women each had
very different views of their relationship. The nail technician was attentively listening and nodding her head
but was completely focused on the task at hand. The
client continually focused on herself, never asking the
nail tech about her personal life. She desired friendship
but didn't really know how to go about acquiring it.
She shared with me that most of her friendships from
childhood and college had dissolved over time, having
been replaced by shallow social media friendships and
work acquaintances. She was lonely but still unaware
of what she was missing out on in her life.

The whole situation boggled my mind, and
although I kept thinking, *This isn't real friendship*, this
beautiful young woman sadly didn't have that same
realization. She was so absorbed in herself that she
didn't realize her relationship with this nail technician
was completely one-sided.

The exchange left me pondering friendship, and
the Holy Spirit has convicted me to begin asking myself
some questions about it: How does one find good
friends? Do I desire only friends who will agree with
me and serve me the way the woman desired the nail
technician to serve her? What kind of friend am I to the
various people in my life? Do I ever become so absorbed
in my own world that I forget there is another person at
the other end of the relationship? Do I exhibit virtuous
behavior in my relationships? Do I turn to the saints as
role models for example and intercession?

I realized that God was working in me to take a deeper look at myself and how I could be a better friend, more like the treasured one presented to us in Sirach 6:5–17. God wanted me to deepen and develop friendships by first starting with my own personal transformation.

Being a good friend requires me to slow down and evaluate what is important in my relationships. I know there have been times when I have been a bad friend to those who are so good to me. I also realize that extending true friendship is more than remembering someone's birthday, texting a quick hello, or meeting up for drinks after work or a long day. While it may include all of those things, at its core, authentic friendship is about figuring out how to allow my God-given relationships to guide me and my friends closer to Christ.

Over the years, I have learned about the gift of true friendship. Good friends bring laughter out of pain, joy out of sorrow, and meaning to life. Friends, *good* friends, show us what it means to be fully alive and help us lighten our loads. Without friends who seek virtue, we can easily lose sight of who we are. As a result, we can become so absorbed in ourselves or worldly things that our views of life become warped, skewed, and even downright selfish. I have seen that when we allow ourselves to be attracted to the wrong people—those who feed our vices and weaknesses—our lives can take a dramatic turn for the worse. We must ask ourselves, "With whom does God want us to be friends?" God is not calling us to have deep and close-knit friendships with everyone, but through the desire to be a better friend to others, we can improve all our relationships and evaluate how much time and energy we should invest in each one.

In addition, we can be better friends by working on basic Christian virtues necessary to friendship and putting another's good before our own. The process of friendship is all about being Christ to others and learning to love and serve God.

As Michele and I travel around speaking about our first book, *Divine Mercy for Moms: Sharing the Lessons of St. Faustina*, women often approach us and share that their favorite part of our talk is about our friendship. We usually kick off the talk by telling about our twenty-year relationship and our favorite quote from John Paul II—"In the designs of Providence, there are no mere coincidences"—since we know that our friendship did not happen by chance but by the grace of God. We realize it is a gift to have faith-filled friends in our lives who support us in our journey and transform us into the women we are today.

Our friendship began at Franciscan University of Steubenville. Over time, it has changed, and more importantly, it has deepened. We have seen God's hand at work in our relationship. Michele met her husband at my wedding and became engaged on my first anniversary. Incredibly, we even had babies on the same day, in the same hospital, just down the hall from each other—on June 8, which happens to be National Best Friends Day. Over the years, we've worked together in many Catholic outreaches, from Catholic radio to our local Catholic Women's Conference, which have led to our writing, speaking, and blogging ministry for Catholic women. God has shown us in a very personal and direct way that good, holy friendships can transform us as well as those we encounter. Thanks to the gift of our friendship, God has been able to bless our work and allow us the time and energy we need to serve our families.

What Is Friendship, and Why Do We Need Friends?—Michele

Recently, my daughter had a fight with one of her friends. In their childish drama, they swore never to speak to each other again. "Why do we need friends anyway?" my daughter remarked. "We have our family, and we have TV."

I had to smile at the comment. I explained to her that no one is perfect and that although friendship is a blessing, it takes some hard work! In fact, Emily and I consider all of our friendships "a work in progress." In addition to each of us wanting to take on the "project" of looking at our inner self and the type of friend we both were, we also titled this book *The Friendship Project* because we know we have to continually work on our friendships or they will dissolve into shallow acquaintances. Not only are having deep and meaningful friendships fun and important parts of our lives, they are needed to keep us healthy and sane. We might think that television and social media can fill our void for friendship, but the fact is that nothing is more valuable than a friend. As St. Augustine writes, "In this world two things are essential: life and friendship. Both should be highly prized and we must not undervalue them. Life and friendship are nature's gifts."[1]

With the advent of social media, people can connect with more friends than ever before; however, research has shown that, compared to twenty-five years ago, Americans have fewer friends to whom they confide. The average dropped from three friends to two; some even reported one friend or none.[2] Having good friends is important to our physical, mental, and spiritual health, yet society ignores its importance.[3]

Friendship has been talked about since ancient history. The famous fourth-century philosopher Aristotle classified friendship in three categories: utility, pleasure, and virtue. The first category is comprised of friendships of utility, meaning our focus is on what we get out of the relationship; think of the nail tech story above. The second type of friendship is one of pleasure, based on our passions and having fun. High school and other young relationships are good examples. The goal is to have as much fun as possible. The third type of friendship is "virtuous friendship." Aristotle even goes so far as to call these forms of friendships "perfect."[4] These friendships form when we wish the best for the other person. Such relationships require work to develop but are well worth the time and effort. They call for the cultivation of a friendship where we can be our true selves and not only have fun with each other but also share the important things in life, like our faith. St. Francis de Sales reminds us,

> Love everyone with a great love of charity, but have friendship with those capable of communicating virtuous things to you. The more exquisite the virtue you put in your exchanges the more perfect will your friendship be. If you share knowledge, your friendship is indeed very praiseworthy; more so, if you communicate virtues, prudence, discretion, fortitude and justice. If your mutual and reciprocal exchange is about charity, devotion, Christian perfection, precious indeed will your friendship be. It will be excellent because it comes from God, excellent because it tends to God, excellent because its bond is God, excellent because it will last eternally in God. How good it is to love on earth as one loves in Heaven, and to learn to cherish one another in this world as we shall do eternally in the next![5]

Since these types of friendships require a significant investment of time and attention in building a trusting relationship, it is impossible to have several virtuous friendships, but they are essential to finding fulfillment in life. Virtues, even in a worldly sense, are recognized by all as qualities needed for happiness. Friendships built around developing virtue attract deeper relationships and awaken our inner souls so that we become better persons. Good friends need to be sought out, cherished, and cultivated.

The saints, too, wrote about the importance of friendship, but they have taken it to a level beyond simple human goodness virtues. They have labeled this next level of friendship "spiritual" or "Christian" friendship. Going deeper into our relationships means inviting God into them and developing friendships that are a "foretaste of heaven." St. Aelred of Rievaulx, a twelfth-century Cistercian abbot, believed that true friendship is based on encouraging each other to love God and neighbor and that "friendship must begin in Christ, continue with Christ, and be perfected by Christ."[6] Likewise, St. Augustine shares with us that everything authentically good in friendships, everything that is true, comes from God, but true spiritual friendship offers us the ability to share in the inner life of the Trinity.[7] Francisco Fernández-Carvajal writes, "Down through the centuries, friendship has been (and still is) a pathway along which many men and women have come close to God and gone to heaven."[8] When Christ is at the center of our friendships, the meaning of these relationships will far outlast the moment and can transform us into saints. When we find friends who are able to share our faith life with us, we will never feel alone.

How Do We Become Better Friends and Develop Spiritual Friendships? Learning about the Virtues and the Saints—Michele and Emily

How do we go about being a good friend and finding good friends? How do we experience this universal need for friendship in a way that is healthy and good for both parties involved? How do we transform our friendships into deeper, more meaningful relationships? How do we view spiritual friendships, and how can we develop them? Emily and I are not perfect and don't have all the answers, but we are going to dive in and investigate this topic. With the help of eight pairs of Catholic saint friends, we will take a deeper look into particular virtues that will help us become better friends and how their spiritual friendships on earth helped them become amazing saints.

A virtue, according to the *Catechism of the Catholic Church*, "is a habitual and firm disposition to do the good. It allows the person not only to perform good acts, but to give the best of himself" (*CCC*, 1803). The virtues are key to helping us change our hearts, and they provide us with the framework we need to make changes in our relationships. We are all in the process of growing, most importantly in relationships with others and God. We need the virtues to help us become the best people we can be and live lives of happiness and holiness. We are all called to be saints by the nature of our Baptism; however, we can't be holy without virtue! When we live virtuous lives, we are in control of our passions. When we are not in control of our passions, our weaknesses are exposed and we are more prone to sin. Our actions and our choices reflect our faith, and when we live lives of virtue, we have joy in living good, moral lives. As St. Paul writes in Philippians 4:8,

"Whatever is true, whatever is honorable, whatever is just, whatever is pure, whatever is lovely, whatever is gracious, if there is any excellence and if there is anything worthy of praise, think about these things." It is not easy to live a virtuous life, but Christ gives us graces to persevere if we ask for them and desire to become holy.

In each chapter, we'll focus on one of the following virtues: faith, hope, charity, prudence, gratitude, loyalty, generosity, and prayerfulness. We'll explore how growing in each virtue will help us become better friends and help us deepen our relationships into spiritual friendships. Included will be a "saint pair": two saints who were friends while on earth. The saints are called so because they lived lives of extraordinary virtue. It was to our great delight to discover that so many saints who walked this earth had spiritual friendships that inspired a deeper relationship with God and helped them become the amazing heroes of virtue for whom they are known. A priest once shared with us that "one saint begets another," and these saints—through their friendships—influenced, mentored, and assisted each other in living lives of heroic virtue. When we allow the right people to influence us and help us, especially in the spiritual world, we can be transformed!

At the end of each chapter, we'll also provide some practical advice and strategies on how to grow in these virtues and implement them into your relationships. With Christ as our key example and the saints as living proof, we can learn a lot about friendship. If you can learn to be a better friend, it will impact the relationships in all areas of your life.

Finding Faith

Sts. Gertrude and Matilda

~Michele~

Faith is the theological virtue by which we believe in God and all that he has said and revealed to us, and that Holy Church proposes for our belief, because he is truth itself. By faith "man freely commits his entire self to God." For this reason the believer seeks to know and do God's will.

—*Catechism of the Catholic Church*, 1814

Going away to college seven hours from home, I didn't know a single person. It was time for me to make a fresh start with my life and make new friends. I quickly made friends with several other girls in my dorm who had attributes I really cared about at the time; they were pretty and popular. We started classes and began hanging out for breakfast, lunch, and dinner as well as the evenings and weekends. We bonded over late nights of celebrating, cramming for exams, watching useless television in our dorm rooms, working out, and playing intramural sports together. While virtues weren't the criteria for selecting my new friends, God had a bigger plan in mind. Most of these girls and I were still fledglings in our faith. We knew from our parents (and the gifts bestowed upon us at our Confirmation) the truth of our Catholic faith, but we hadn't fully embraced the lifestyle. Thankfully, my parents and their parents had the gift of a strong faith. They had intentionally sent us to a university where that gift would be set alive and nurtured.

In this unique environment, we all began to grow. One by one, we each had a spiritual awakening and discovered a personal relationship with Jesus Christ. Collectively, we made our faith the priority in our lives. Perhaps the most significant development in our early college careers was our decision to join the household system. These groups of men and women were small, Christ-centered, Spirit-led communities. The goal of these "Catholic sororities" was to help each student develop deep friendships with other students and to grow in body, mind, and spirit by supporting one another and holding one another accountable during their conversion process.[1] Providentially, my household included Emily and was named after the Blessed Mother, Mary: "Mother of Love."

Our household met each week to break bread together on Saturday during small prayer services we held in common areas of the dorms. There, we learned to pray with our friends. This was the first time some of us had ever prayed aloud with anyone besides our family members. We went to Mass together, played sports together, were roommates, and grew to be almost as close as sisters. Our friendships and our faith continued to deepen over the years. As we grew, we noticed that these friendships were different than others that we had experienced in the past because they were deeply rooted in our faith: our belief in God and the teachings of the Church. Through our faith-filled friendships, we encouraged each other to seek out the will of God for our lives and held each other accountable for our actions.

Four short years after we met, this group of sisters in Christ graduated from college and moved all over the country. Although miles separated us, our friendships remained strong. We stayed in touch through an e-mail group I initiated shortly after graduation and had many reasons to reunite. We were bridesmaids in one another's weddings, became godparents to one another's children, and continued to visit and call each other often. As our families grew, we visited one another and vacationed together. Over the years, our children have come to know one another and have continued our friendships into the next generation.

When there were no more weddings to attend, we started getting together every few years for a just girls' reunion to reconnect and catch up. One of the highlights of the reunion weekends was going to Mass together. We would all sit together in one long pew, just as we had in college. During our most recent get-together, I looked down the pew and thanked God that each of us had taken that tiny seed of faith that was planted in us and allowed it to blossom. We have all matured into women of faith, making our faith a priority in our lives, and our friendships are stronger than ever. Now we are active parish or Catholic community members spanning from Ohio; Texas; Georgia; New York; Vermont; Illinois; Washington, DC; Iowa; to Canada. The virtue of faith has given us such a strong bond that distance cannot separate us from one another. Though we live in a world that no longer embraces Judeo-Christian values, I appreciate these friendships of faith. I am blessed to know that I can always call upon these women for support in times of need and encouragement in living out our Catholic beliefs.

While my college relationships were the first strong friendships I had with women who exemplified the virtue of faith, they were certainly not the last. Although I was in a unique environment in college before, I realized I could also have a strong community of faith-filled friends in my life now by belonging to a small faith-sharing group. When I was first invited to my friend Chrissy's home for a women's Bible study, I didn't feel like I was "in the market" for any new friends. I was satisfied with my current friendships, busy with my job, and happily married. In hindsight, I see that this was one of the best things that could have ever happened to me, as it was a beautiful opportunity to make new friends in faith. After college, as I desired to grow stronger in my own faith, I realized it was essential for me to seek out women who felt the same. In this way, we became a support system for each other in a world that does not embrace a Christian lifestyle.

The first night of the study, seven of us, including Emily, sat around Chrissy's kitchen table, and we began studying the scriptures. We met twice a month during that study, and each week a new friend joined us. After we finished that study, we progressed to another in the series, and our group continued to grow. This went on for years! Since many of us had young children then, we also met in each other's homes for "Rosary playdates," where we'd let the kids play and enjoy each other's company before gathering to pray the Rosary. We added a Christmas party to include our spouses and, later, a family picnic in the fall. We instituted a group e-mail that provided a way for us to communicate meeting times and served as a prayer chain list. It also was a safe place for us to ask questions about our faith and parenting, share great articles on the faith, and suggest other faith-building opportunities and events. Even though we lived in different parts of the city and belonged to different parishes, the common bond built by a search for truth and a deeper relationship with God kept us cemented together.

Our group continued to grow as we met new women who longed for companionship and the support of a small community. To this day, we come together to celebrate good times: new babies, Baptisms, First Communions, graduations, and new jobs. We offer support for each other in hard times too: the loss of parents, troubled marriages, job losses, serious illnesses, miscarriages, and once, even the heartbreaking sudden death of a newborn. Over the years, we've performed works of mercy together, reaching out to others outside of our group, such as hosting a baby shower for a woman in a crisis pregnancy, running a vacation Bible school for underprivileged kids, collecting Easter baskets and Christmas gifts for homeless children, and hosting food drives for a local food pantry.

Our mutual support continues to be both physical and spiritual. We create care calendars for new babies or those who are going through a difficult time. Most importantly, with one quick e-mail, these forty women are immediately praying for a pressing need or intention. While we don't live together as I did with my household sisters in college, the community of friendship we have created is very similar in its spiritual underpinnings and the faith that bonds us to one another. Many of these women are my closest friends, including Emily, who is my former household sister, my longtime Bible study companion, and now my partner in ministry!

The Virtue of Faith

Faith is believing in God and giving him our yes to his will in our lives. Faith is not only believing in God but also experiencing him and seeing the world through his eyes.[2] St. Paul writes in the letter to the Hebrews, "Faith is the realization of what is hoped for and evidence of things not seen" (11:1). The virtue of faith is one of the three theological virtues—the other two are hope and love—and is a gift "infused by God into the souls of the faithful" (CCC, 1813) at our Baptism. They are theological because they "relate directly to God. They dispose Christians to live in a relationship with the Holy Trinity. They have the One and Triune God for their origin, motive, and object" (CCC, 1812). Having faith changes everything. When we have faith, we place God first in our lives. Having faith is the foundation of all the elements in Christianity; it is the bedrock of our hope, our love, all the virtues, and even our prayer.[3]

By practicing the gift of our faith, especially through the reception of the sacraments, we can open up this gift and allow it to spread into our lives and all of our relationships. Being open to faith is the first step in building spiritual friendships. We need faith to allow Christ to work in our lives. We read in the gospels that Jesus could not perform miracles in Nazareth because of their lack of faith. However, in many other instances, Jesus was able to heal illness, raise people from the dead, and even forgive their sins because of their great faith. "Your faith has saved you; go in peace," he told the sinful woman who washed his feet with her own hair in the Gospel of Luke (7:50).

Holy friendships are key to growing in the virtue of faith. Without the right support system and faith-filled friendships, living your faith is more difficult. St. Teresa of Avila writes that spiritual friendship is so extremely important that: "I don't know how to urge it enough. It is necessary for those who serve Him to become shields for one another that they might advance."[4]

Our journey as Christians is not one we are meant to travel alone. Jesus himself had many friends while he was on earth, and as he sent out his disciples to spread the Good News, he sent them out "two by two" (Mk 6:7). In the book of Ecclesiastes we are reminded, "Two are better than one. . . . If the one falls, the other will help the fallen one" (Eccl 4:9–10). When I have been weakened by sin, my friends have been there to pull me up and help me continue on in faith. My friends of faith are the people in my life who encourage me to take the higher road and, by their example, help me grow closer to God. After encountering these women, I am always inspired to live out my faith more fully. Their influence may be through praying with me over a cup of coffee or sharing a blog post on how to raise children in the faith. It may be an invitation to meet them at Mass or to attend an event featuring an inspirational Catholic speaker. It can even be as simple as a text message with a scripture verse, encouraging me to stay strong and reminding me that God loves me. These friendships are a gift to me and help me in my daily walk as a daughter of God.

The goal of spiritual friendships is to encourage each other on the journey, grow in holiness, and do God's will in our lives. By doing so, we can know, love, and serve God in this lifetime and, ultimately, live by the words of St. Padre Pio: "Let us become saints so that after having been together on earth, we may be

together in Heaven."[5] In this way, our friendships will
last forever! When two people have the common bond
of friendship in God, not only can a strong relationship develop but also their love of God can change the
world.

Friendship of the Saints: Matilda and Gertrude

Throughout history we have seen that many of these
holy men and women had friends who helped them
in their journeys toward heaven. Through these spiritual friendships, both people not only grew in their
faith but bore such a witness that they are now pub-
licly recognized by the Catholic Church for their heroic
virtue. Some of these friendships were so strong that
they have even been depicted in Catholic artwork. A
few months ago, a friend sent me a text message with
a picture of two saints standing beneath Jesus with his
Sacred Heart exposed. The caption beneath the picture
read, "St. Matilda instructing the novice, St. Gertrude."
I was familiar with St. Gertrude the Great's powerful
prayer to release holy souls in purgatory, but who was
this other saint in the picture? I did some research and
found the story of two beautiful women and how the
faith of St. Matilda, also known as St. Mechtilde, was
shared in their friendship. This grace helped St. Gertrude to become truly great in the eyes of the Lord.

St. Matilda was born in 1241 in Saxony (now Germany). She joined the Benedictine order at a young age
and had many gifts that made her an attractive, holy
person. She was bright and talented. A gifted singer,
she was given the duty of directing the choir. She had a
very sweet disposition with a personality so kind and
genuine that everyone wanted to be around her. Pope
Benedict XVI spoke about Matilda in an audience in

2010, stating she was "distinguished by her humility, her fervor, her friendliness."[6] It was noted that no one left her company without being consoled and strengthened. Matilda was like a mother to all she met, and she was a gifted teacher as well. When she spoke about the Word of God, students would gather around her as if she were a preacher. She was placed in charge of the school at the monastery, and it was in this capacity that she first met St. Gertrude.

According to the common practice of that time, Gertrude came to be a student at the monastery at the age of five. She was put in the care of Matilda, who was then twenty years old. Gertrude became a disciple of Matilda, but as Gertrude matured, their relationship deepened and they became confidantes and close friends. Gertrude, like her mentor friend, was a strong student and possessed many spiritual gifts. Most importantly, Matilda taught Gertrude the faith and helped Gertrude understand the spiritual gifts they both had been given. Gertrude had a deep conversion of heart at about the age of twenty and went from a life that focused on studies to one of deep, mystical prayer. Gertrude knew the gift of her faith was due to her friendship with Matilda and wrote in her memoirs to Jesus, "I would have behaved like a pagan . . . in spite of desiring you since childhood, that is since my fifth year of age, when I went to live in the Benedictine shrine of religion to be educated among your most devout friends,"[7] a time which included the influence and friendship of Matilda. Matilda, who was also a mystic, had a unique influence on Gertrude because of their friendship, and she helped Gertrude navigate her faith journey as the young woman grew closer to Jesus, showing her that the gifts she was given were from God. With Matilda by her side, Gertrude's mysticism deepened and she received the spiritual or invisible stigmata. While Gertrude had no physical evidence of the wounds of Christ in her hands and feet, she felt the pain interiorly.

With both of their eyes fixed on the Lord, the friendship of the two saints deepened and strengthened over the years. When Matilda was about fifty years old, she went through a very serious spiritual crisis and physical illness.[8] She confided to Gertrude and another friend all the special gifts God had given her. They kept notes of these special graces, and the notes were later published as *The Book of Special Grace* (also called *The Revelations of St. Matilda*). Later, the two saints coauthored a book, *Prayers of St. Gertrude and St. Mechtilde of the Order of St. Benedict*, which can still be purchased today.

Matilda died of natural causes on November 19, 1298, at Helfta monastery, yet her friendship with Gertrude continued even after Matilda departed from earth. After her death, Matilda appeared to Gertrude and told her that *The Book of Special Grace* was her greatest joy and that it would bring much glory to God and good to those who read it. Gertrude lived only four more years, but even in that short time, her example of a holy life inspired many. She wrote *The Herald of Divine Love* as well as her *Spiritual Exercises*, which have been called "a rare jewel of mystical spiritual literature."[9] The writings of these women have been described as "incomparable treasures" on the doctrine of the Sacred Heart of Jesus. Gertrude is the only woman among the saints to be called "the Great."

The friendship of Gertrude and Matilda is an example of how the faith of both women was deepened throughout their lives because of their relationship. Their positive influence on each other encouraged both of them to draw closer to God and to know his will in their lives. Both of these saints' lives were changed forever by their friendship, which continues today in heaven. Their faith inspires many women today as the story of their holiness continues to be shared throughout the ages; their friendship is an illustration of how our friendships of faith can help us become saints too.

Obstacles to Faith

Living a life of faith is not always easy. Skepticism, doubt, secularism, and hard teachings of the Church can cause our faith to be shaken. Living out faith is also different than just accepting our beliefs. It requires us to act according to our belief systems, rooted in love, and to bear fruit. We can believe in God and the teachings of the Church, but unless this belief changes our lives, our faith is dead. A person of faith resembles Christ. Pope Francis reminds us that "Being Christian is not just obeying orders but means being in Christ, thinking like him, acting like him, loving like him; it means letting him take possession of our life and change it, transform it and free it from the darkness of evil and sin."[10] A life of faith is not an easy ride, and therefore it requires perseverance through suffering and trials. In persevering, we remember the words of St. Paul to the Corinthians to "stand firm in the faith, be courageous, be strong" (1 Cor 16:13).

In addition to the ordinary difficulties of living a life of faith, we can also reject this gift or lose it through sin. Although I had these faith-filled friendships, there were times in my life that my selfish desires were more important than God's will and my friends' encouragement. At times, I fell into sinful patterns that were hard to break. At those times, I knew my choices were sinful, but I didn't have faith strong enough to walk down the narrow path and I continued to fall. Through the gift of Confession and the blessing of faith-filled friendships,

I was able to work through my struggles. I found the support system I needed to become the daughter of God he was calling me to be. Our heavenly Father wants us all to come to him for this healing and, if we ask him for this grace, he will provide for us the opportunities to develop the gift of increased faith. We need these special graces to persevere! We cannot do it on our own. If you struggle with this virtue, recall these promises of Jesus in Matthew 7:7–11:

> Ask and it will be given to you; seek and you will find; knock and the door will be opened to you. For everyone who asks, receives; and the one who seeks, finds; and to the one who knocks, the door will be opened. Which one of you would hand his son a stone when he asks for a loaf of bread, or a snake when he asks for a fish? If you then, who are wicked, know how to give good gifts to your children, how much more will your heavenly Father give good things to those who ask him.

If we ask, God will also bless us with faith-filled friends in our lives. So many friends have shared with me, as they were beginning to grow in their faith, that they asked God to send new friends into their lives who were also his friends. They were shocked at the new friendships that they soon encountered. God wants to give us this gift so we may grow, with our friends, in our faith and come to deeply know him, love him, and serve him. When two people have this common bond of friendship in God, not only can a strong relationship develop but, together, their love of God can change the world.

*Friendship in Progress: Developing and Deepening
Friendships of Faith*

Starting a small faith-sharing group or joining one isn't the only way to grow in the virtue of faith or to build faith-filled friendships. Meeting new friends can be a daunting task, especially if you have never had a relationship that incorporated faith, but in time these friendships will be your most treasured ones. In a day and age when we all have different schedules and family situations, consider some of these options:

1. *Introduce yourself to someone at Mass.* What better place to meet someone who is trying to build the virtue of faith? Invite someone you meet at Mass to coffee or an event to get to know her better. One of the best things that ever happened to me was when a young mom reached out to me after Mass one day and invited me to her home for a playgroup. Her son was just a few months younger than my son, and we ended up meeting every other week. This relationship encouraged me to attend daily Mass more often to meet her there. After Mass, we had an opportunity to talk and spend time together while the boys played.

2. *Attend a Catholic women's conference or retreat.* These day- or weekend-long events offer a time of renewal of faith as well as a chance to connect with old friends, deepen our relationships with acquaintances, or meet new friends. Our conference in Columbus, Ohio, draws women from several surrounding states. Make it a trip with friends (or soon-to-be friends), carpool together, and spend the day being refreshed by Catholic speakers and the sacraments. Afterward, celebrate the day by going to dinner together to discuss what you experienced.

3. *Join a parish-based women's or moms' group.* If your parish doesn't offer one, check out the other parishes in your diocese or consider starting your own. Oftentimes, these groups can offer many different types of opportunities for fellowship, fun, and invitations to grow deeper in your faith. I was recently asked to help form a moms' group for some parishes in our area and have been blessed with many new friendships of faith.

4. *Identify women in your life to meet with to grow and deepen faith friendships.* Many times our friendships do not grow because we do not invest the time we need to get to know the person more deeply. We may feel the initial attraction of friendship, but unless we deliberately spend time strengthening our friendships and getting to know the person more intimately, we end up with many "strong acquaintances" versus true friends. Emily and I designate each Friday as "Friendship Friday" and spend part of that day with one friend we desire to grow in our relationship with or with whom we have lost our connection. When you are open to the promptings of the Holy Spirit, he will show you whom to pursue.

5. *Pray for an increase of faith for you and your friends.* St. Matilda and St. Gertrude understood the blessing of friendships. They prayed for each other and even wrote several "prayers for friends" in their prayer book. By praying for faith, we come to see and know God's will in our lives and help our friends do the same. By modeling the lives of the saints who were friends and asking for their intercession before the throne of God, we too can become better friends and grow in holiness.

   Pray with us:

Come Holy Spirit, deepen my faith in you.
Come Holy Spirit, show me how to be a friend of faith.
Come Holy Spirit, bring me friendships of faith.
Sts. Gertrude and Matilda, pray for us.

2

Holding on to Hope

Sts. Perpetua and Felicity

~ Emily ~

Hope is the theological virtue by which we desire the kingdom of heaven and eternal life as our happiness, placing our trust in Christ's promises and relying not on our own strength, but on the help of the grace of the Holy Spirit.

—*Catechism of the Catholic Church*, 1817

Often when we're at speaking engagements, Michele and I reference a powerful life experience that changed both of us forever: our first experience with a close friend being diagnosed with cancer. I still remember the shock when I was told that our friend from college, Stacey, had Stage III brain cancer. She was a young mother in her early thirties with two children under the age of four. Stage III cancer does not bear a happy prognosis, and despite having an amazing support system, Stacey was given only eighteen months to live. She and her husband quickly set out to find the best doctor and seek counsel on when and where to receive treatment and prepare for this great battle. Her journey was like that of many others who fight this terrible disease. However, for Stacey, it was especially painful having her young children witness their mother's battle for her life.

Long before her cancer diagnosis, Stacey was an ambassador of hope. It was evident in all aspects of her life, including her love for Christ and his Church, and her authentic belief in others, evidenced by her large circle of friends, whom she would often inspire to be their best. Stacey and I not only bonded by being in the same household during college, but we were also elected to student government together, lived down the hall from each other, played intramural sports together, and spent countless hours having fun together. Everyone who knows her has a Stacey story because she always manages to make a remarkably lasting impression on the people around her. Hope is life-giving and always leaves us wanting more of it!

Throughout Stacey's life, she has allowed her hope in Christ to lead her along the path. I have witnessed firsthand how she brought joy and life to suffering souls, whether they were complete strangers or dear friends of hers. One of Stacey's best qualities is the big smile that's always on her face. She assumes the best of others and never harbors negative feelings. She's a breath of fresh air to those she encounters. People of hope are attractive, no matter what trials they're enduring, and they make for great friends.

It was a hard pill for me to swallow—seeing such an amazing friend and person go through this daunting and difficult trial. Before this I had always believed that if you were a good person, nothing bad would happen to you; this was the first time in my life I experienced the suffering of a close friend. Thankfully, as Catholics, we see the value in our suffering, which can be used to purify the soul and strengthen us on our journey to heaven: "For this momentary light affliction is producing for us an eternal weight of glory beyond all comparison" (2 Cor 4:17). While Stacey's experience wasn't a light affliction, it was an example of a human suffering that was significant and life changing for her whole family. Ironically, the things that caused her tremendous suffering actually brought her closer to Christ and her loved ones. With this diagnosis came a greater appreciation for each breath she took, her family, her friends, and her faith. She lived the scripture from Romans 12:12: "Rejoice in hope, endure in affliction, persevere in prayer." As longtime friends, Michele and I wanted to be there for her, but we lived far away and had young children and budding careers that left us with little free time and limited resources. We knew we needed to do *something*, but we didn't know what.

At first, I struggled with how to concretely help my friend as she fought for her life, until one day a little package arrived in the mail that reset my perspective. Two friends of ours living in Washington, DC, made all of our college friends matching rosary bracelets as a way to remind us to pray for Stacey. These packages went out across the country to inspire all of us to pray and petition the Lord for the graces she needed to remain hopeful and be healed.

I am certain my other college sisters would agree that these bracelets united us spiritually and brought some light to the dark situation. We wore these bracelets with reverence daily and knew that God was in control, no matter what happened. Every time my prayer brace-let bumped up against the kitchen counter or got caught on my clothing, I was reminded to pray for my friend. I began to step outside of myself and my own struggles spiritually and think of this young mom as she fought the battle for her life. The experience was a powerful witness to how when we pray for others, we grow in our faith and change our lives from the inside out. Personally, I grew as a Christian by learning to pray for someone else. Praying for Stacey taught me how to step outside of my own life, as consuming as it was then, and develop a prayer life that was on behalf of someone else. I prayed for her specific needs, not only mine. As a result, I slowly saw a transformation taking place within me. My faith ignited as I learned to pray for my friend who was thousands of miles away from me but close to my heart. I became more of a hope-filled person as I witnessed this virtue in my friend. Since this experience, I see the value of praying for others, believing that God is always providing healing—especially spiritually—when we are open to it. We also share our journey toward heaven each and every day.

Our support did not end with prayer; it began with it. We were all inspired to send additional expressions of our love and support for Stacey and her family. We sent her packages, gift cards, and letters, and many of our college friends visited her. We all went out of our way to show that we were thinking of her, even if she didn't have the energy to respond to each one of our little actions. By showing her love in these little ways, we were able to bring hope to Stacey when she needed it most, just as she had inspired us for years. With her hope-filled presence, Stacey spurred us on to be better wives, mothers, friends, and most importantly, daughters of God. It was a gift to be a source of inspiration and a prayer support to a friend in need, and I learned that hope is a virtue well worth cultivating and spreading to others.

I am happy to say that Stacey is approaching her tenth anniversary of being a cancer survivor—a real victory! Recently, Stacey shared with Michele and me her doctor's words: "We don't know why some people beat this type of cancer while others don't; we can have the same cancer in two different people, and it can take one as a victim and the other can be a survivor." She has not only shown us that with God, all things are possible, such as fighting this deadly cancer, but she has also been a witness to how to do it in a godly way.

Ironically, whenever we embrace our crosses in life and give our struggles back to Christ, amazing fruits come from our pain. Tragedies are always opportunities to bring people together, ignite faith in those who have lost it, and witness to the power of Jesus Christ and how he is here to guide us. Even to this day, Stacey thanks God for the blessings that have come from her cancer: the strengthening of her marriage, an increasing appreciation of her children, and most importantly, the deepening of her faith in God and growing love for him. I still believe that Stacey knows how to have more fun than anyone else I have ever met. Her ability to live out the virtue of hope keeps her pointed toward heaven. Her example of keeping her sense of humor, optimistic spirit, and joyful personality only illuminated her desire to fight disease. She focused on living to have more time on earth to do the will of God. This was inspiring and made me want to be more like her. Cancer did not hold her back from living her life but, rather, ignited her love for life and her faith. It is a reminder to us all that hope makes a lasting impact on our daily lives and provides us with an eternal perspective.

The Virtue of Hope

Hope is the greatest gift you can give someone. In 1 Peter 1:13, we are instructed to "set [our] hopes completely on the grace to be brought to [us] at the revelation of Jesus Christ." This definition has nothing to do with wishful thinking but, rather, focuses on trust in Jesus. Those who practice the virtue of hope recognize the need to trust in Christ and not the world. They are not just hoping for heaven like a child hopes for a snow day but, rather, "know" it is going to happen. Hope is a virtue that empowers us, especially when we experience dark times in life. This virtue grounds us so that we can see past the trials that cloud our minds and darken our souls. It is what provides us the vision for our ultimate and final goal: heaven. It is always difficult to witness someone suffering, especially a family member or friend, but when we offer them Christian hope, we are able to help them gain an eternal perspective on their suffering. The reality is that we will all die someday, but the closer we become to Christ, the more empathetic we are to others' suffering and the softer our hearts become.

When I am personally suffering, I need to know that this experience has value like Christ's crucifixion. Suffering is where faith is transformed from a sentimental belief system to a life support machine that can stabilize souls and preserve them from discouragement. In the midst of suffering, we can only experience true happiness when we place our trust in Christ. Stacey's cancer was an opportunity to grow closer to Christ and receive tremendous redemptive graces for herself, her family, and indeed, all whom she encountered as she offered her pain up with Christ. As Christians, our suffering has power. A negative person may call it a punishment or a death sentence and see the suffering as an end, but a hopeful Christian sees it as a means to holiness.

When we choose to love others and be a source of hope and support in difficult and dark moments in life, we gain wisdom. Our perspective, so often focused on the self, is forever expanded to include others. We are able to walk with them and see that suffering with Christ has value. It transforms our hearts, especially when walking the painful road with a friend. Hope is what prepares us for the heavenly banquet, no matter what our final moments on earth consist of. Hope is the set of wings that carries us to heaven. We read in Philippians 3:20 that "our citizenship is in heaven, and from it we also await a savior, the Lord Jesus Christ."

Without hope we are weak, broken, depressed, and doubting, and we can ultimately be crushed by the weight of our own weakness, no matter how trivial or grave the trial. If we are not willing to bring hope to our friends and learn how to cultivate this virtue in ourselves, we are missing out on what it means to be a Christian friend. Hope helps us deal with our own difficulties, joyfully trust in God's will, and inspire others to trust God as well.

Friendship of the Saints: Perpetua and Felicity

One of the most striking testimonies of hope dates back to the very beginning of the Church. In Eucharistic Prayer I in the Mass,[1] we invoke the intercession of two powerful witnesses to Christ: Sts. Perpetua and Felicity, whose feast day is the seventh of March. The account we have of them comes from a diary written by Perpetua herself and is one of the earliest writings by a Christian woman. While awaiting her death in prison with her friends and fellow Christians, Perpetua wrote this account. The story was completed by eyewitnesses after her death. Her testimony reads like a fiction novel with action, drama, and inspiring feats of courage.

Vibia Perpetua, a twenty-two-year-old mother of a young child, lived as an upper-class, well-to-do woman. Her love for Christ motivated her to cross social and cultural barriers, proclaiming her love for Christ and her willingness to live out the consequences of this radical Christian religion. Perpetua boldly decided to become a Christian, despite knowing that she could be put to death under the Roman emperor Septimius Severus. He persecuted Christians who refused to worship the emperor and Roman gods. Felicity and Perpetua's friendship began when Felicity was her personal slave, and the relationship blossomed into a spiritual friendship that would help them support each other during their imprisonment and the final moments leading up to their martyrdom.

St. Perpetua's most cherished gift was being baptized a Christian, infusing the virtue of hope into her soul. Her Christian baptism provided her with the graces she needed to give a holy witness through dying a martyr's death so that future generations could worship freely. She even declared that during the time of her baptism, she heard God's voice, and the message she received was to pray only for endurance in the face of severe trials.

When St. Perpetua was arrested and tried for being a Christian, her family desperately wanted her to renounce her Christian faith and return to her old way of living. Her father even said, "Daughter . . . have pity on my grey head—have pity on me your father, if I deserve to be called your father, if I have favored you above all your brothers, if I have raised you to reach this prime of your life. Do not abandon me to be the reproach of men. Think of your brothers, think of your mother and your aunt, think of your child, who will not be able to live once you are gone. Give up your pride! You will destroy all of us! None of us will ever be able to speak freely again if anything happens to you."[2]

Despite her parents' pleas to deny her faith, St. Perpetua declared to her father, "I cannot be called anything other than what I am, a Christian."[3] Her faith could not be shaken. The pressure this young woman must have felt, with a father's plea to give up the faith! His argument was strong and he even reminded her of her maternal responsibilities. The judge also pleaded with her to change her mind, as he did not want to see this young woman die. Yet her hope in Jesus, in the face of difficulty, helped her remain strong.

Imagine hearing about Perpetua, a young mother in her early twenties with an infant, and Felicity, pregnant with a baby girl who would be born in the cell mere days before she died. Perpetua and Felicity were willing to sacrifice their motherhood in order not to deny Christ.

Perpetua and Felicity were martyred in the coliseum in Carthage in honor of Caesar's birthday. Their gruesome death started with humiliation, harassment, and torture by wild animals, and then finally, their throats were slit. St. Perpetua's parting words were, "Stand fast in the faith and love one another."[4] These saints and martyrs stood strong in their faith, even refusing to wear the gown of the gods, declaring that they freely died for Christ, so should be permitted to wear what they wanted at their execution. Their spiritual friendship was short-lived yet deeply rooted in their love for Christ. They inspired each other to strive for greatness and never to lose hope, which is essential to have as a Christian in a broken world, especially during the most horrific trials and tribulations. These women shared a journey that was so dramatic and unbelievable that few women could remain unmoved by their heartfelt witness and courage. Their story inspires and reminds us that hope is a virtue worth seeking.

These two third-century saints and martyrs, St. Perpetua and St. Felicity, have made a lasting impression on the world through their courageous witness to their love for Christ[5] and their brutal martyrdom, which is historically documented in the diary of St. Perpetua.[6] Not only did they die together on the same day but their friendship was their greatest blessing in the final days leading up to their deaths.[7] They are a powerful example of the spiritual sisterhood in Christ that is possible between women of different social status and walks of life. They are indicative of St. Paul's words: "We know that all things work for the good for those who love God, who are called according to his purpose" (Rom 8:28). These friends are a source of inspiration for us today.

Being a Friend of Hope

Above, you heard about two amazing saints who allowed the virtue of hope to transform their final days on earth and be a source of inspiration for generations to come. I also shared with you my dear friend's remarkable story of how her hope while battling cancer was pivotal in being a survivor and is one of her most attractive qualities. When she was first diagnosed, she shared with us that "hope for me lay in the fact that I truly believed Christ could heal me, whether it was a physical healing or a spiritual healing." She went on to share that in a moment of desperate prayer the day she received the news of her cancer, she asked that Christ lead her to a friend who had been down this road before. He gave her the image of himself in the Garden of Gethsemane, covered in blood-stained sweat, and told her *he* had been there, *he* knew what it was like to have that fear and feel that pain, and she should put her hope in him. He also gave her an overwhelming feeling of peace, and she felt Christ's hands surrounding her and knew she could accept the outcome of this diagnosis, no matter what it was.

Discussing her cancer battle, Stacey went as far as to say, "I would do it all over again: I appreciate my family, I try to enjoy each day I have to live, and the Lord brought my husband to Confession and a deeper level of faith because of my illness. I never lost hope that Christ would heal me, use me, and allow me to touch the lives of others. This time of my life was difficult, to say the least, but the reality is that only through suffering do we encounter what it means to be alive!"

When you encounter a person of hope, you will not forget it; you want to breathe in the air they breathe, bottle it up for later, and spread it to others. Hope is contagious when it is grounded in our Christian faith, and no matter how hard the imposter of secular optimism tries, it has no weight or value compared to the virtue of hope. Pope Francis shares with us that "Hope does not let us down—the hope of the Lord! How often in our life do hopes vanish, how often do the expectations we have in our heart come to nothing!"[8]

As Christians, we must be resolute in hope and not toss this virtue out the window and start to fret and fear the world when the going gets rough. We must never focus on the darkness that surrounds us and forget that Christ is there to constantly guide us and lead us!

As friends, we need to bring hope to each other. Hope is for everyone, not just our spiritual friends; therefore, we must inspire non-Christian friends to seek Christ and his boundless love. Hope is about creating an attitude toward life that is inspiring, joyful, and optimistic because no matter what difficult twists our stories take, they always end with the victory of Christ. Philippians 2:9–11 says, "God greatly exalted [Jesus] and bestowed on him the name that is above every name, that at the name of Jesus every knee should bend, of those in heaven and on earth and under the earth, and every tongue confess that Jesus Christ is Lord, to the glory of God the Father." We are called to believe this truth; every knee shall bend and confess that Jesus is Lord. In this dark culture, it is difficult to imagine, and yet with the virtue of hope, we can put our trust in our Lord that this scripture will ring true. We can trust our Savior and encourage our friends to do the same.

Hope is what should always separate us from non-Christians, as we know there is more to the story of life than what meets the eye. Imagine your friends, family, coworkers, enemies, and complete strangers all worshiping Christ in his glory; hope is what allows us to want this for everyone! It is almost too much for the mind to comprehend, especially in this very secular world. The scriptures are clear: "every tongue [will] confess that Jesus Christ is Lord." With that in mind, we are called to spread hope to others: even the hopeless, especially the hopeless. Imagine being able to see good in everything that is tossed, flung, smeared, or spattered our way!

As women, we have the innate ability to believe in others and often cheer for the underdog. We love a great story of transformation or success, and even a miraculous account of healing or improvement. This natural gift of hope can go dull in a dark world. We can hide our hope or allow it to be diluted by others. Yet if we choose to live it, this virtue will stand out and remind our friends and ourselves of God's love. Remember: hope without prayer is useless, but hope with prayer is powerful! Pope Francis shares with us that we need to have an attitude that is hopeful:

> "Anyone who is a man or a woman of hope—the great hope that faith gives us—knows that even in the midst of difficulties God acts and surprises us." We cannot have hope if we do not have faith that God can and will act in our life. He will take our dirty messed up life and allow it to be transformed for the Kingdom. He allowed people to be transformed from the inside out or the outside in. Hope is contagious, it is radical, it is worth developing and being that person that is cheering on friends to never lose their faith and be strengthened by hope.[9]

Obstacles to Hope

Hope is the beacon of light that guides us and gets our lives back on track to prepare us for heaven. The *Catechism of the Catholic Church* refers to two types of sins against hope, namely, despair and presumption. Regarding the former, the *Catechism* states, "man ceases to hope for his personal salvation from God, for help in attaining it or for the forgiveness of his sins. Despair is contrary to God's goodness, to his justice—for the Lord is faithful to his promises—and to his mercy" (*CCC*, 2091). About the latter, presumption, the *Catechism* posits, "man presumes upon his own capacities . . . or he presumes upon God's almighty power or his mercy" (*CCC*, 2092).

As Christians, we are called to put all of our trust in Christ and never despair of the outcome we foresee or presume that we know best. Hope and trust in God are deeply linked. When we seek out God's plan for our lives and trust in Christ, there can be no room for despair, despite how difficult a situation may appear. Christ has laid out a path for each and every one of us and wants to give us the graces we need to remain faithful to God's will. In Romans 15:13, we read, "May the God of hope fill you with all joy and peace in believing, so that you may abound in hope by the power of the Holy Spirit." Consider asking the Holy Spirit to cast his light on your life and prepare, strengthen, and help you on your path to heaven.

Looking back over the course of my life, I find there have been many friends and family members to whom I failed to spread hope, instead causing hurt and harm through my silence. I didn't show up in any way, shape, or form as a person of hope, which is what they needed during difficult times in their lives. God gave me specific opportunities to make a difference when they were encountering darkness, and instead, I did nothing. Of course I wanted to send a card of support, I wanted to pray for them and help them, yet I didn't because "life just got in the way." I forgot to ask Christ for the necessary graces I needed and instead relied on my own strength to do the good works I desired to do. I presumed that I could live this life on my own, that I could do it by the power of my own free will. I couldn't.

Recently, God has allowed me to see that it is never too late to live out this virtue and correct my ways. Life is not over, and I can always choose to turn back to Christ. Being a good Christian friend is not about living in the guilt of what we should or could have done. Rather, Christ has set us free to be people who trust in our divine Savior. This is a real source of joy!

So if you are thinking of friends, family members, and colleagues who could have benefited from your actions, words, and prayers, especially in spreading the virtue of hope, consider being a source of this virtue now! I often feel I should apologize to others for times I wasn't hope for them. Doing this brings healing. Turn over a new leaf, and remember that Christ is always there for us, longing to lighten our loads spiritually, emotionally, and physically. He doesn't want us to be overwhelmed by this world but, rather, see that our true destination is heaven.

Friendship in Progress: Developing and Deepening Friendships of Hope

1. *Join a ministry at church that helps bring hope.* Some ideas are to become a eucharistic minister for the sick and homebound, join a welcoming committee, help with youth ministry, or join a social justice committee such as St. Vincent de Paul. By meeting like-minded, hopeful people through volunteer work, you will meet new friends and provide meaningful moments to others.
2. *Reach out to someone who is suffering or going through a difficult time.* There have been many instances in my life when I have made new friends because someone whom I did not know (or know well) reached out to me when I was in a difficult situation. Sometimes I just needed a listening ear. When you reach out, don't give advice; instead, just listen and be a beacon of hope. Offer to pray for this person daily in a special way.
3. *Ask the Holy Spirit to show you the person he wants you to befriend.* Sts. Perpetua and Felicity broke through cultural and socioeconomic barriers and developed a spiritual friendship that continues into eternity.

You may be surprised at who the Holy Spirit will bring into your life, especially if you are willing to look outside your comfort zone for new friends.

4. *Focus on being a beacon of hope to your friends.* Be deliberate about being hopeful; try to break negative habits, especially when speaking about your problems and the problems of the world. When you find yourself heading down a path of negativity, deliberately stop yourself. As Christians we are called to realize that there is hope for everyone! We are called to first and foremost believe that Christ can work miracles in other people's lives, much like he did in Stacey's life; our job is to pray for these miracles to happen: "For nothing will be impossible for God" (Lk 1:37).

5. *Share an aspect of your faith with a friend who needs encouragement.* Send a prayer card, an encouraging text, or a scripture verse to someone going through a difficult time. This can open a door for more conversation and a deeper friendship.

6. *Pray for an increase of hope for yourself and the friends in your life.* Recently, I have begun to pray a powerful prayer that has allowed me to see Christ active in my life in a whole new way. I have asked him to help me be a person of hope and see that Christ can transform anything and bring new life out of what is dead and desolate. When I lack hope I pray, "Dear God, please turn my ashes into blessings." This simple prayer is one you can say over and over again and see that whatever you have burned to nothing (in other words, turned into ashes) can be transformed and made new again. This pertains to all of the areas of our lives.

    Pray with us:

Come Holy Spirit, deepen my hope in you.
Come Holy Spirit, show me how to be a friend of
   hope.
Come Holy Spirit, bring me friends of hope.
Sts. Perpetua and Felicity, pray for us.

3

Cultivating Charity

St. Thérèse of Lisieux and Servant of God Léonie Martin

~Michele~

> Charity is the theological virtue by which we love
> God above all things for his own sake, and our neigh-
> bor as ourselves for the love of God.
>
> —*Catechism of the Catholic Church*, 1822

A few years ago I was experiencing some health issues.
I had kept this private, so I was surprised when I saw
this text message from my friend Maria: "I know this is
random, but would you guys eat Puerto Rican shredded
pork and yellow rice? I made too much."

It was 7 p.m., and the ground beef I envisioned
making into dinner was still frozen on the countertop.

I was exhausted, weak, and not feeling well. Making dinner was the last thing I wanted to do. I immediately texted Maria back and accepted the offer, sharing what a godsend it was. I didn't tell her what was going on but said I would share when I stopped by to pick up the meal. As I drove, I could hardly believe I was receiving this gift from a friend who was so in tune with what God was calling her to do that she thought of me in the midst of a busy evening with her own family. A friend who didn't realize I was hurting but who took the time out to love and offer me a gift that I needed more than she knew. Her response to God's call to love me, even when she didn't know I was in need, filled my broken heart with joy.

When I pulled up, she asked how I was doing. As I relayed the details of the past twenty-four hours, I told her how much it meant to me that she reached out in this simple yet profound gesture and what a consolation her friendship was to me.

"It must have been the Holy Spirit," she replied as she handed me the dinner. "What else can I do for you?" It was like Jesus was standing there at my car window saying, "I am here with you; I have not abandoned you; I love you." I could feel the presence of Christ the Healer, and my heart jumped into the arms of love reaching out to me in a terrible time when I was hurting, sad, and in pain.

I had experienced these arms before, the strong arms that held me up when my son was paralyzed in the hospital for more than a month, when my daughter was diagnosed with a rare genetic condition, when our family experienced the loss of a loved one, and during many other difficult times when my friends reached out in charity to help me. At those times, Christ's love was palpable through the actions of my friends.

I have found during the trials of my life that God's love embraced me through the gift of my friends, who loved me when times were tough. Those friends allowed the love of God to pour out through them and put my needs before their own. St. Catherine of Siena writes in her *Dialogue* how God uses us to share his love with others: "I could easily have created men possessed of all that they should need for both body and soul, but I wish that one should need each other and that they should be my ministers to administer the graces and gifts that they have received from me. . . . I have made man my ministers . . . in order that they may make use of the virtue of love."[1]

God constantly calls us to love. Scripture reminds us of this numerous times. In John 13:34 we read, "I give you a new commandment: love one another. As I have loved you, so you also should love one another." In 1 Peter 4:8 we read, "Above all, let your love for one another be intense, because love covers a multitude of sins," and in 1 John 3:11, "For this is the message you have heard from the beginning: we should love one another." Yet we live in a world where empathy is on the decline and narcissism is on the rise.[2] Due to growth in social isolation, we are becoming less loving, less generous, less willing to walk a mile in the other's shoes. I am sometimes shocked at what I read between "friends" on social media these days. Instead of love, we give criticism, gossip, and sometimes, even hatred.

To be true friends, we must practice and grow in the virtue of charity (love). Also infused at Baptism like faith and hope, charity grows as we practice acts of love to our neighbors. Charity is not a feeling but rather a direct act of the will that transforms us. St. Albert the Great writes, "If, then, we possess charity, we possess God, for 'God is Charity' (1 Jn 4:8)."[3] According to the

Catechism of the Catholic Church, "it is the *form of the virtues.* . . . It is the source and the goal of their Christian practice. Charity upholds and purifies our human ability to love, and raises it to the supernatural perfection of divine love" (*CCC*, 1827). It is the virtue that inspires a life of self-giving. Although I have always realized the importance of charity, desiring it is not enough. Charity requires practice fueled by prayer to obtain the graces I need to live out this virtue.

Charity is the most important virtue, the most superior, and the virtue that inspires all the others. The scriptures teach us a great deal about charity. We read in 1 Corinthians 13:13, "So faith, hope, love remain, these three; but the greatest of these is love." Jesus himself taught us about love through his preaching and exemplified it with his life. When asked the greatest of the commandments, Jesus replied, "The first is this: 'Hear, O Israel! The Lord our God is Lord alone! You shall love the Lord your God with all your heart, with all your soul, with all your mind, and with all your strength.' The second is this: 'You shall love your neighbor as yourself.' There is no other commandment greater than these" (Mk 12:29–31). Jesus' greatest act of love was when he laid down his life for us on the Cross, so that we might have eternal life.

One of the most popular scriptures on love is found in 1 Corinthians 13:4–8. Although it is oftentimes thought of only in instances of romantic love, St. Paul wrote it for every relationship! It describes what love is and what it isn't: "Love is patient, love is kind. It is not jealous, it is not pompous, it is not inflated, it is not rude, it does not seek its own interests, it is not quick tempered, it does not brood over injury, it does not rejoice over wrongdoing but rejoices with the truth.

It bears all things, believes all things, hopes all things, endures all things. Love never fails."

Can you imagine a friend who is perfect in love? One who is kind, patient, and looking out for your best interests? One who is even-tempered, forgiving, and never failing? What a goal to strive for, to be a friend of love! St. Aelred of Rievaulx writes, "The source and origin of friendship is love. Although love can exist without friendship, friendship cannot exist without love."[4] If we all chose to love like Christ loved us and to be completely selfless, our world would be a different place. Yet as much as we desire to live the virtue of love, it is so hard! Many things can prevent us from loving: our own egos, our indifference, and even our busyness can get in the way of loving. I can think of many situations when I have failed to love others, especially those who are closest to me. St. Teresa of Calcutta once wrote, "It is easy to love people far away. It is not always easy to love those close to us."[5] It's sometimes easier for me to love my neighbors who live across the world by making a donation in my mercy jar and feeding the poor in Africa than it is to reach out to the friend who I know is lonely and find the time to spend with her. Loving is an unselfish act of the will, and many times it involves a sacrifice.

Love is the virtue that guides us into becoming saints. If we want to grow in this virtue, St. Teresa of Avila writes, "Beg our Lord to give you this perfect love of neighbor. . . . He will give you more than you know how to desire."[6] By being a friend of love, we can be the hands and feet of Christ here on earth and, most importantly, help our friends get to heaven.

Friendship of the Saints: Thérèse of Lisieux and Léonie Martin

One of the most popular saints of modern times is St. Thérèse of Lisieux. Her family was so extraordinary that not only has she been canonized, but her parents, Sts. Louis and Zélie Martin, were declared saints on October 18, 2015, and the cause of canonization has been opened for her sister Léonie, giving her the title Servant of God. Our life's example can help lead others to holiness, and that case is certainly made in this family! With the model of her parents, St. Thérèse was able to climb the spiritual ladder of holiness, and through her friendship with her sister Léonie, Thérèse's spirituality was the spark that inspired Léonie to achieve a life of heroic virtue.

St. Thérèse was born in France in 1873 to Sts. Louis and Zélie Martin as the youngest of nine children. Only five of them, all girls, survived into adulthood. Thérèse's mother died when she was only four, and her sisters Marie, Pauline, Léonie, and Celine cared for her. As a little girl, she was spoiled and had an overly sensitive personality; however, at the age of fourteen, she had what she describes as a "Christmas conversion" and overcame her hypersensitivity. This allowed her to ignore the small, petty things she was overly concerned with and enabled her instead to embrace the true crosses in her life with joy. Then she retrained her sensitivity to be a gift to God and to be used for his work. This special favor from God showed Thérèse that he was working miracles in the everyday, the ordinary, and this understanding of God's actions was to become the story of her life and her spirituality. After receiving this grace, Thérèse rapidly grew spiritually and soon desired to join the convent. Although initially denied because of her young age, she made a pilgrimage to

Rome and petitioned Pope Leo XIII, who, after listening to her plea, said, "Go, go, you will enter if God wills it."[7] She became a Carmelite sister on April 9, 1888, at the young age of fifteen. She lived a cloistered life and was known for her exemplary love. She is known for her motto, "the little way," which entails doing little things with great love for others. She knew she was a little soul and could never do great deeds; as she wrote in her autobiography, *Story of a Soul*, "The only way I can prove my love is by scattering flowers and these flowers are every little sacrifice, every glance and word, and the doing of the least actions for love."[8] Her life was characterized by making sacrifices and loving those she didn't even like.

St. Thérèse knew she was little and had many faults, and she knew she could never be like many of the great saints. However, she also knew God would not put the desire to be a saint in her heart if it could not be fulfilled, so she looked for a new way to climb heights of holiness, in spite of her littleness. She writes in *Story of a Soul*, "So I sought in holy Scripture some idea of what this life I wanted would be, and I read these words: 'Whosoever is a little one, come to me.' It is your arms, Jesus, that are the lift to carry me to heaven. And so there is no need for me to grow up: I must stay little and become less and less."[9] She lived a simple life of love and died from tuberculosis at the young age of twenty-four. On her deathbed, she promised to spend her heaven helping those on earth. Although her life seemed unremarkable, her writings were copied and distributed to many convents. Her little way inspired many ordinary people to live extraordinary lives of holiness and love. She was canonized in 1925.

One of those who were greatly inspired by her writings was Thérèse's sister Léonie. Although St. Thérèse is the most well-known of the Martin daughters, all of the Martin daughters joined the convent, including Léonie, who was nine years older than Thérèse. Léonie had a difficult childhood and was very ill as a baby. Her illness continued into her girlhood, and it is said there are very few pictures of her as a young girl because she had a terrible eczema that exuded pus that covered her body. She suffered abuse from a servant, had been expelled from school because her intelligence was "low," and even felt isolated from her own family.[10] She was the middle child and seemed to be the odd one out; however, her mother wrote she had a heart of gold.[11] She was disobedient and unruly, and the death of her mother made things more difficult for her. However, she and her sisters cared for St. Thérèse in the absence of their mother. Thérèse wrote of her special relationship with Léonie in her autobiography: "Léonie has also a very warm place in my heart. She loves me very much and her love was returned. In the evening when she came home from school she used to take care of me while the others went out, and it seems to me that I can still hear the sweet songs she sang to put me to sleep."[12]

When Thérèse entered the convent, she continued her relationship with Léonie and the two often exchanged letters. Thérèse always encouraged Léonie. Léonie had tried three times to join the convent, but she left each time. Before Thérèse died, she shared, "After my death I will cause Léonie to return to the Visitation, and she will stay there."[13] Léonie persevered, and after her saintly sister died, she attempted to enter the convent again by becoming a disciple of the little way, living with trust and abandonment to God. She again went to the Monastery of the Visitation of Caen, and as her sister promised, she stayed. Léonie finally made her vows on July 2, 1900, and said it was the happiest day of her life.

The love and the friendship of the sisters was so deep that after the death of Thérèse but before Léonie made her vows, Léonie wrote her other three sisters, Marie, Pauline, and Celine, who were in the convent at Carmel, saying, "Our little Thérèse has shown me that she is continually by my side by means of a strength which motivates me in everything I do."[14] One of the few items Léonie was able to keep in her cell was a picture of Thérèse. The little way transformed Léonie into a peaceful, cheerful sister who enjoyed serving. Of all the Martin sisters, it is said that Léonie understood and lived out St. Thérèse's spirituality the best.[15] Léonie died on June 17, 1941, and as Thérèse predicted, she "stayed at the monastery" as she was buried in the Visitation crypt, despite Pauline's desire for all the Martin sisters to be buried under the shrine of Thérèse. After Léonie's death she was almost forgotten, but soon letters began to pour into the convent asking her intercession or thanking her for favors received. Her cause for canonization was opened in 2015.

Obstacles to Love

The story of Thérèse and Léonie is a beautiful one that even transcended death. Thérèse's love for her sister was so great and their friendship so true, she only wanted to help her sister to become a saint. Not only did her life of love inspire her sister but it can also inspire us to live charitably and encourage our friends to do the same. In our friendships, we should always work to be loving. St. Thérèse writes, "Charity should not only be a matter of feeling but should show itself in deeds."[16]

As women, we can become hard of heart and lose sight of how we should treat others. One sin against love that we can easily find ourselves in is gossip. Pope Francis has spoken about the importance of avoiding gossip, because these words, which can at first be seen as nice or amusing, are really a poison that can "kill the reputation of the other person."[17] He goes on to share that if we avoid gossiping we can become holy! We should all strive to take the more beautiful path of love. Jesus offers us the answer: to love instead as "love is the only measure that has no measure, to move past judgments."[18] St. Teresa of Calcutta reminds us that words can tear down or build up: "The quickest and surest way towards thoughtfulness is the 'tongue'—use it for the good of others. . . . 'From the abundance of the heart the mouth speaks.' If your heart is full of love, you will speak of love."

It can be hard to avoid gossip or to ask our friends not to speak negatively about others; however, St. Thérèse of Lisieux shares a beautiful story in her spiritual diary about a close friend and a sister in the convent. Initially, a real friendship developed and helped them grow spiritually, but soon she realized their conversations turned toward gossip. St. Thérèse prayed that God would use her to speak and enlighten her friend. In a loving way, Thérèse spoke with the sister and embraced her, and their tears mingled. The other sister realized her fault, repented, and began a new life. From that point on, their friendship was strengthened and truly spiritual.

Another barrier to charity is selfishness or pride. Personally, I have fallen into this sin when I am too wrapped up in my own little world and become blind to my lack of charity. God will sometimes show us our shortcomings and how we have hurt our friends, sometimes without trying. This recently happened to me. Emily and I were speaking at an out-of-state event.

A friend heard we would be in the area and traveled more than an hour to hear us. I was very honored by the gesture. After speaking on the works of mercy and giving in deed, word, and prayer to others in need, we were approached by our friend at our book table. She shared how she always brought a meal to friends in need because, at one point in her life, her daughter had surgery and only two friends reached out to her in this difficult time. Now, understanding how it felt to be left alone in difficult situations, she always reached out in love. My first reaction was one of shock. *What terrible friends you have!* was the first thought that went through my head. Yet as the old saying goes, "when you point a finger at someone else, there are three pointing back at you!" Although this friend moved, I knew about the surgery and her difficulty yet had not reached out. I wasn't intentionally trying to hurt her, but I was too wrapped up in my own little life and didn't even think I should send some love! God even prompted me, making it easy for me to reach out, as by chance (or God-incidence) I happened to run into a mutual friend at the grocery store who was headed to visit our friend, bring groceries, and help babysit. I could have sent a few things up with her—even a simple dessert or snacks—yet I was too absorbed in my own little world to even offer.

Thankfully, my friend did not harbor negative feelings toward me and our friendship is still intact; however, I can tell you many stories of friendships that were ruined because a friend did not reach out when the other was in need. How many times do we hold grudges over little things, which not only ruin friendships but also hold us back spiritually?

Whether the offense against us was intentional or not, we also need to be careful of hypersensitivity. Our sensitive nature is a gift from God, but when we are overly sensitive, like St. Thérèse was as a child, that sensitivity stems from self-centeredness and self-love instead of love of the other. Alice von Hildebrand writes, "A sensitive heart is given to us to feel for others, and to love them more deeply and more tenderly. But since original sin, it tends to degenerate into a maudlin self-centeredness that is not only disastrous but also causes great pain for the sensitive person. However, thanks to prayer and grace, the Christian is given the means of purifying his sensitivity, so that his heart will resemble more and more the Heart of the God-Man, the Sacred Heart."[19] As a sensitive person, I have often-times overreacted and felt very offended by the slightest comment, finding myself in tears over even the least criticism. I am learning, with the gift of grace, to assume the best intentions of the other person and not allow the perceived slight to destroy the friendship.

Envy is also a sin against charity and can ruin friendships. When we are jealous of what our friends have, we can poison our relationships. In this day and age, we can be especially prone to envy as we are constantly barraged with images of the perfect kitchen, perfect children, and the "Pinterest-perfect life." As women, we are prone to comparison and competition. The only solution to envy is charity. We should appreciate "the gifts and the quality of our brothers and sisters in our communities"[20] and be happy for our friends instead of jealous. Pope Francis advises, "When I am jealous, I must say to the Lord: 'Thank you, Lord, for you have given this to that person.'"[21] By breathing that prayer when we feel jealousy creeping in, we pray, practice, and persevere.

When we lack charity or someone is uncharitable toward us, we must also remember the fruit of charity:

mercy. Jesus calls us to be "merciful just as your Father is merciful" (Lk 6:36). Seeking forgiveness when we have hurt others and letting go of grudges when our friends ask (and even when they don't ask!) for forgiveness is a very difficult thing to do. Seeking out the sacrament of Penance is also an important way to grow in charity. As God has forgiven us, we can in turn learn to forgive others.

St. Ambrose reminds us to "preserve, then, my sons, that friendship you have begun . . . for nothing in the world is more beautiful than that. It is indeed a comfort in this life to have one to whom you can open your heart, with whom you can share confidences, and to whom you can entrust the secrets of your heart. It is a comfort to have a trusty man by your side, who will rejoice with you in prosperity, sympathize in troubles, encourage in persecution."[22]

Friendship in Progress: Developing and Deepening Friendships of Love

1. *Do a work of mercy together with a friend.* When we reach out to others, especially strangers, we grow in love. Ideas for works of mercy are at www.divine-mercyformoms.com.

2. *Take time out to examine your shortcomings that prevent you from loving your friends.* Are you selfish with your time? Do you lose your patience too easily? Are you "too busy" to give to a friend in need? Are you overly critical, jealous, or gossipy? Are you overly sensitive? Whatever is holding you back, ask God for the grace to overcome it and make an effort to avoid this sin.

3. *Seek the forgiveness of a friend whom you have hurt.* Send a letter or an e-mail or make a phone call to mend the rift. She may not forgive or maybe she has

already forgiven you, but asking for forgiveness will free you from the past and give you peace. Hopefully your friendship can be restored!

4. *Go out of your way to do an act of love for a friend.* It doesn't have to be expensive: bake some cookies, bring over coffee, and spend some time with a friend today who might need a little pick-me-up. Like my friend did at the beginning of this chapter, listen to the Holy Spirit and see whom God is calling you to reach out to!

5. *Pray for an increase in the virtue of charity and that we help our friends grow in love.*

    Pray with us:

    Come Holy Spirit, deepen my love for you.
    Come Holy Spirit, show me how to be a friend of love.
    Come Holy Spirit, bring me friends of love.
    St. Thérèse of Lisieux and Servant of God Léonie Martin pray for us.

4

Practicing Prudence

St. Hildegard of Bingen and Bl. Jutta

~Emily~

Prudence is the virtue that disposes practical reason to discern our true good in every circumstance and to choose the right means of achieving it.

—*Catechism of the Catholic Church*, 1806

I was clenched in a ball, crying my eyes out; all I could do was beg the Lord to help me reset my life. Despite my best efforts, what I was doing was not working for anyone in my family. We needed to start over, but I had no idea how I was going to do it. I had been homeschooling my children for more than eight years, but the thrill and excitement had worn off. In the earlier years, homeschooling was a time of great joy and discovery that helped me foster an amazing relationship with my children. As the years progressed, however, preparing lessons for numerous kids at different grade levels and working to fit everything into the day had caused my stress to mount and my relationships with my children to become tense. In the end, I had six children under the age of thirteen who literally needed me day and night. I would run around trying to meet everyone's needs, and yet I was constantly so overwhelmed and guilt-stricken that I was underperforming not only as their educator but as their mother as well. I consistently found myself drowning in laundry, dishes, chores, and schooling.

My passion and love for my family and my Catholic faith had led me down this road. Although rooted in good intentions, if things continued down this path, the result would be more harmful than grace-filled. My homeschooling lifestyle made me feel trapped in my own home and left very little time for others. I was doing, doing, doing, and I had forgotten many of the important relationships that had filled my life outside of my own walls. The many wonderful friendships I had spent a lifetime developing were slowly slipping away, soon to be casualties of my self-inflicted isolation. I had cut out one of the very things from which I found meaning and enjoyment: my friends. I stopped going to Bible study so I could clean up after a long day; I turned down coffee with my girlfriends or outings to celebrate birthdays because of the needs of my children; and sadly, even the idea of a trip away with my husband seemed unattainable. I was slipping into my own version of motherhood instead of what God wanted for me.

Looking back, I realize I was missing a critical quality that would have helped me through my trial—the virtue of prudence. This virtue can fish us out of the sea of uncertainty and guide us away from trouble like a lighthouse preventing us from getting dashed upon the rocky shores of life. My lack of prudence had caused me to lose my way in the darkness.

Eventually, I hit a breaking point. It was time to seek guidance on how to dig myself out from the lifestyle that I had once loved but now exhausted me. There was someone in my life who had been offering that guidance, but I had been too proud and self-absorbed to notice. My husband had been gently telling me that I was taking on too much and burning myself out, but I'd chosen to take it as criticism rather than the honest concern for my well-being. I had been faking my own invincibility and needed to open up to him about my troubles. When I finally did, I was relieved to find that he was more than willing to look into other options for schooling and promised to support me however he could.

My first thought was to put the kids in Catholic schools, but I immediately reasoned that it would be far too expensive, especially considering we had five school-aged children. I then considered sending them to public school, but I thought the transition from homeschool to public school would be very harsh on the children since they had been so sheltered. No matter what I considered, I always found a way to sabotage the idea without ever making a truly concerted effort to study it with an open mind. I felt weak, overwhelmed, and in need of wisdom and support. Throughout this ordeal, I had tried turning to God in prayer, but to be honest, my prayers were all too often focused on asking for help without listening for his subtle replies. As I struggled on, though, I began to hear his calls to reconnect with others.

I realized that many of the key relationships that had slipped away were the very ones I needed for support and counsel. I began to open my heart and share with other friends and family members what was really going on. This required a big dose of humility. In the end, I discovered that nearly everyone was happy to support me and offer helpful advice. As I began working through my concerns, thoughts, and feelings with those who cared about me, my options became clearer and my outlook more hopeful. I realized that others were also concerned and that my real friends wanted to help me but didn't know how. I needed to take the first step; I needed to be open to change. And then it happened.

Often, when we are in need and are open to change, God will send one of his followers to guide us during our difficult times. In my case, God must have known that I needed something obvious because he sent a deacon friend of mine, who also happens to be the father of my oldest son's boyhood playmate, with a gentle invitation to consider a small Catholic school at his parish. As a matter of fact, it wasn't the first time he had reached out to us. Year after year he had made similar welcoming gestures and encouraged us to check it out, but I had been too mired in my life to pay much notice. This time, I listened. When we did finally respond and check into it, I was relieved to find that the principal of this school welcomed my family with remarkable kindness. We reworked our budget and were able to bring this new stage in our life to fruition. Through the grace of God, we found a way to pay for the education of now six kids at Catholic schools. God can and will speak through your friends, and they can be a real source of strength and wisdom when you are open and honest.

I am so thankful that friends and family came to my aid by intervening in a helpful way and being part of the solution instead of fueling the flames with gossip, slander, or discourse. In life it is easy to choose targets for our conversation if they appear to be weak, vulnerable, or even different. I feared that I would be criticized if I admitted that I had failed at homeschooling. It was hard for me to ask for help because I had to first admit to even myself that I *needed* help. People looked up to me as the woman who formed the homeschool support group and a leader in the community, but by making a change I was afraid I would be looked down upon.

True friends challenge us to make changes in our lives and do not just nod in agreement with everything we think, say, and do.

True friends care and act, just as my deacon friend had done. I experienced the important reality that prudence protects us from burnout and becoming too zealous in areas where Christ isn't asking us to perform. Yes, life is difficult at times, but when we have a lifeboat waiting for us and we choose to ignore it, life only becomes more challenging. Prudence can ultimately protect us from confusing what we expect of ourselves with what Christ is asking. "Come to me, all you who labor and are burdened, and I will give you rest. Take my yoke upon you and learn from me, for I am meek and humble of heart; and you will find rest for yourselves. For my yoke is easy, and my burden light" (Mt 11:28–30). God's ways are gentle and the burden he gives us feels light, not like the chain I felt around my neck. Christ wants to take away our burdens.

The Virtue of Prudence

Prudence is about "smart living."[1] We practice prudence when we slow down enough to evaluate how we are actually going to live our lives. Prudence is a virtue that can't be infused into us like the theological virtues— faith, hope, and charity—were at our Baptism. Instead, we need to work hard with the help of God to acquire it. For a virtue is a "habitual and firm disposition to do the good."[2] Being the first of the cardinal virtues, prudence applies to all the aspects of our lives so we can grow in sound judgment. The *Catechism* states, "It is called *auriga virtutum* (the charioteer of the virtues); it guides the other virtues by setting rule and measure. It is prudence that immediately guides the judgment of conscience" (CCC, 1806). With the help of this virtue, all of our relationships will improve, for prudence guides a person to take abstract moral principles and apply them to daily life and circumstances.[3] St. Augustine teaches us that prudence is "the love that distinguishes what helps us to go towards God from what hinders us."[4]

The Three Aspects of Prudence

St. Thomas Aquinas shares three aspects or steps to prudence.[5] I am certain I would have benefited if I had worked through these steps years ago. Making a prudent decision isn't just about choosing "right over wrong" or even choosing a "good over another good."[6] With this in mind, here are some guidelines that can help you make better decisions.

The first stage of making a prudent decision is focusing on self-evaluation, seeking out counsel or deliberation on what you are deciding. This stage is about gathering information and seeking out your options. It is important that we seek others outside of ourselves and gather all the necessary information to make a decision. St. Josemaría Escrivá shares with us that "to be prudent the first step is to acknowledge our own limitations, so we must look for advice—but not advice from just anyone. We go to someone who has the right qualities, to someone who wants to love God as sincerely as we do and who tries to follow him faithfully."[7]

When making a decision, we need to slow down enough to determine the factors that play into it. We need first to humbly acknowledge our limitations and second to find someone who is qualified to give advice. We need to ask the Holy Spirit to reveal people in our lives who love God, follow a Christian lifestyle, and have trustworthy advice. This also means we don't just troll the Internet or talk to friends with the same perspective and who already agree with us. True counsel takes place when we are willing to be honest with our reality and limitations and see a situation from a different perspective. That is why, if you are the friend giving this type of counsel, it is important to be honest and realize that you can help shape and form another person's conscience. It is important that we mindfully map out our decisions so that we develop a plan for success. This aspect of prudence takes time and energy but is well worth the investment. Maybe that is why instructing the ignorant is a work of mercy; the Church is affirming that we are called to help others in forming their conscience and determining where their time, talent, and energy should be placed.[8]

The second stage is making a smart judgment.[9] After we seek counsel and look at the facts, we make a judgment based on our reality and what God is saying to us. A commonality of being Christian is that we all desire to follow Christ—but our situations can be vastly different. The key to making a decision is to avoid making it based on our fears but rather in pursuit of the freedom and liberation Christ has won for us. The question should be, *What is Christ calling me to do?* Prudence is about figuring out what God wants from us and formulating a solid plan for success based on the first stage of counsel. The key to formulating a good judgment is trusting in God's will for us and our families and finding peace with our decisions. When friends seek our counsel, we are called to support others and not impose our will on them, especially if we have not taken any time to pray and discern on their behalf.

The third aspect of the virtue of prudence is decisiveness: living out your decision.[10] We must make a decision and go with it; when we second-guess ourselves, we just spin our wheels. How many of us are good at gathering the facts and praying about our decisions, but we don't ever act on God's will? We are called to be decisive when we are practicing our Catholic faith, and Christ will reward us for attempting to do the will of God. Fr. Francisco Fernández-Carvajal shares that "following Our Lord means living a life of small and great acts of madness as is always the case where true love is concerned."[11] Just think of the first Christians who went out of their way to spread the Gospel; this resulted in many tribulations for them, and sometimes even death, but they wanted to share the message of Jesus Christ. To the world, our behavior might look mad, but when we are living out the virtue of prudence, we keep our end goal of heaven in mind, rather than self-preservation.

These three aspects of prudence can greatly impact our ability to live out our Catholic faith and help evaluate what is best for our eternal soul. If you follow these steps, you will see Christ's hand in your life in a whole new way and likewise help others work through difficult matters in their life. A priest once told me that God isn't like a game show host who looks at the guest and says, "You picked the wrong door; you lose." All the doors are winners; God will work with us if we do our best to be prudent and prayerful about our lives. In hindsight, I know that my family and I received many tremendous blessings from homeschooling. I thought I was doing God's will, and indeed I may very well have been early on, but I know now that we stuck with it too long. If I would have practiced this formula from the beginning and reconsidered things periodically, my situation would have inspired me to tour schools earlier! This formula is not a one-time cure; as your life changes, you might need to go through the steps again to discern whether your earlier decision is still the *best* decision. Now that I am out of it, I know that walking the difficult road of homeschooling was used by God for his glory, but that is true with all our imperfections. However, it would be even better had I initially made a prudent decision so God could have used me to the fullest.

Scripture tells us that prudence and wisdom go together. Proverbs 8:12 states that "I, Wisdom, dwell with prudence, and useful knowledge I have." Wisdom and prudence lead to knowledge on when to act and what to do. Ironically, the prudent person might appear to be a fool in the eyes of the world for following her conscience and beliefs, for being willing to place God's commandments over the wishes of a neighbor or the government.[12] The prudent person can be led to do heroic things for Christ that might appear to be grandiose, awkward, politically incorrect, or even socially detrimental. Such examples can include not advancing a career choice because of moral or spiritual conflicts and beliefs or being open to life and not practicing contraception in a marriage. Prudence is always a virtue that guides us toward our greatest good, and when we combine it with wisdom, we increase our knowledge on how to live our lives.

Friendship of the Saints: Hildegard of Bingen and Jutta

These women are not well known to modern society, but their witness for Christ and influence on others have made a lasting impact on society. St. Hildegard and Bl. Jutta's friendship was a means to glorify God and renew the Church of the Middle Ages.

Bl. Jutta of Sponheim was born in Disibodenberg, Germany, in the twelfth century. She became seriously ill as a child and promised God that if she was healed she would live a holy life. She was cured and, at the age of twenty, became an anchoress, a woman who withdraws from the world to live a life of prayer. She founded a monastery at Disibodenberg and was known for her wisdom and ability to heal others. People traveled from all over to see her and to seek her spiritual guidance and counsel.

Bl. Jutta played a monumental role in the life of one of the most important women of the Middle Ages, St. Hildegard of Bingen. Hildegard was the youngest child of a noble couple who lived near the southern bank of the Rhine not far from Mainz, Germany.[13] The couple had ten children and gave the youngest, Hildegard, to Jutta to raise at around the age of eight. Her parents saw that God had blessed this young child with unique spiritual gifts—including a mysticism by which she began having visions of God at the age of three. Her parents desired that those gifts be cultivated for the Lord. This child ended up being Jutta's companion and pupil for life, and Bl. Jutta served as Hildegard's role model and spiritual mentor. Most importantly, she was also a dear friend. She taught Hildegard how to read Latin, chant the Divine Office, and play the psaltery, a medieval instrument similar to a dulcimer that is plucked.[14] Hildegard saw all things in the light of God through the five senses: sight, hearing, taste, smell, and touch.[15] She shared these revelations with Bl. Jutta, who also experienced visions and so was able to spiritually mentor to her. This time together shaped Hildegard and allowed her to grow in her spiritual gifts and be affirmed that they were from God. Other women joined Jutta and Hildegard, and the hermitage later became a Benedictine convent. Jutta instructed Hildegard until she died in 1136, and St. Hildegard served as the prioress of the abbey after Bl. Jutta's death. Although Hildegard's fame and accomplishments overshadowed Jutta's, it is believed she was able to achieve such great spiritual and academic loftiness because Jutta was her guide. St. Hildegard said, "Jutta was like a river with many tributaries, overflowing with the grace of God."[16]

St. Hildegard was truly a woman of leadership and left a lasting impact on society. She was an abbess, artist, author, composer, mystic, pharmacist, poet, preacher, and theologian. Hildegard's wisdom was so great that she even advised bishops, popes, and kings. "In her many writings Hildegard dedicated herself exclusively to explaining divine revelation and making God known in the clarity of his love."[17] She would address simple people, religious, theologians, bishops, popes, and government leaders. Pope Benedict XVI wrote that St. Hildegard "expressed the most noble values of womanhood" and proclaimed her a saint and Doctor of the Church in 2012. "She calls us to look beyond the everyday but to value it at the same time. She calls us to see that order in the world is a good thing but it has to be reflective of a virtuous order, a life lived rightly in community."[18]

Prudence can be a wonderful virtue to aid us in developing spiritual friendships and relationships, much like the friendship of St. Hildegard and Bl. Jutta.

These saints allowed their love for God to be the root of their friendship, and they sought each other's wisdom, inspiring each other to grow in holiness. This virtue is essential in all relationships, for it guides us on where to place our time, talent, and energy. If prudence is all about smart living, these saintly examples inspire us to seek out friendships with others who will help us develop a vibrant and fulfilling life doing God's will. As the spiritual director of St. Hildegard, Bl. Jutta helped her friend discover God's will in her life and maximize her time and talents for the Lord while always investing in a deep and rich prayer life.

Prudence and Friendship

Prudence is essential in all of our relationships, and yet it is rarely talked about. Prudence allows us to ask the right questions before moving forward. The proper use of this virtue dictates that we pause and consider what God would want us to do, not what we want to do for God. We must put aside our own egos and objectives and ask ourselves, "Is this my will or his will?" It helps us to use reason and to act rightly in any given situation. The *Catechism* states that prudence "is the virtue that disposes practical reason to discern our true good in every circumstance and to choose the right means to achieving it. . . . It guides the other virtues by setting rule and measure" (*CCC*, 1806). Put simply, prudence is the virtue that enables us to respond fully to direction and guidance from the Lord. What could be better than allowing this virtue to help us evaluate our friendships and decide how to develop spiritual friendships?

Friendship is a two-way street. Both friends need to decide that this relationship is one worth investing in. Prudence can help us determine which friends are right for us to invest in more deeply at this moment in our lives. Through the inspiration of these two saints, we learn that Christ-centered friendships should inspire us to do God's will in our lives and live to the fullest.

To Have Friends, You Need to Be a Good Friend

In life we can have too many things going on at once that pull us away from the people close to us. We can be so busy doing good things that we can be spread thin like butter. Just because something is good doesn't mean that we should do it! I imagine that as a spiritual mentor, Bl. Jutta helped St. Hildegard manage her many interests. When we lack prudence in our decisions, we become so busy that we start dropping balls—and the first things to go are our relationships: our friendships and relationships with our family members. A prudent person makes wise decisions about her time and puts her relationships first. People are more important than things, even the really important things that we feel obligated to do, and how we treat others matters.

When we take time out to figure out our goals for the day, month, or year we can evaluate where our friends lie. It is one thing to say we value our relationships, but when we make little to no effort to see or communicate with them, we are sending conflicting messages. This may be a sign that we need to reevaluate our priorities. We can't show love to others when we are not even in their lives. When I was struggling with homeschooling, a close friend of mine gave me great advice. Part of my problem was that I was a Type A–doer who expected to accomplish way too much in one day. I wrote a list of what I hoped to get done and what I actually accomplished and found that my expectations were really off. This simple exercise revealed that I was so overbooked that there was very little time for others based on my expectations of myself. Prudence allows us to reset our personal expectations and make room for others. Jesus doesn't need more "doers for the sake of doing"; he needs people doing the work he has asked us to do so we can grow in holiness. He needs joy-filled Christians who know that his yoke is light and doable; through prudence and prayer, this is possible.

When we isolate ourselves, we become lonely. Sadly, it is said that one in four Americans are lonely.[19] I personally believe the numbers are higher than that. Are some of us lonely because we don't have significant relationships in our lives or we expect more from others than they can provide? Prudence can help us determine the sources of loneliness and seek the counsel we need to develop meaningful relationships.

One way to develop prudence is to set goals for yourself, stick to these goals, and make sure that busyness doesn't prevent you from being fully alive.[20] One of the real gifts prudence adds is freeing yourself from "survival mode"; rather, you will have a planned formula to follow for success. Set goals for spending time with your friends and keep them; if you plan to have coffee with a friend, set up a date so this happens. Mark your calendar if your goal is to send birthday cards so that you actually do it or even drop a note in the mail to let your friend know you are thinking of them. If a friend has moved away, make an effort to have phone dates or even an annual gathering. Setting goals regarding your friends and following through with them will allow you to develop lasting and meaningful friendships.

Obstacles to Prudence

St. Thomas also shares that sudden, non-prudent behaviors can result when we are led by impulse, passion, or stubbornness. These three pitfalls can also prevent us from being good friends. How many times do we overreact, lash out, and gossip because we have allowed imprudent behaviors to guide our lives? I can recall countless times when my emotions, passions, and impulses prevented me from being a good friend!

The impulsive person doesn't think through a situation. People led by their passions can easily get caught up in emotions and forget reasonable limitations, allowing themselves to be easily swayed by others. When we are stubborn, there isn't much room for the Holy Spirit to direct us, so we are not open to change and are not able to receive the counsel and instruction we need to make prudent decisions.[21] The best way to counter these pitfalls to prudence is to make sure you leave time and energy to pray about your decisions and follow the prudence formula mentioned earlier in this chapter. Consider saying a novena—nine days of prayers strung together offered for a specific intention—or remembering this specific decision in your prayers throughout your day. If you struggle with this, pray to be less impulsive and more prone to act in a prudent manner. Prayer will impact your ability to be prudent.

Not only useful for managing time and being a friend, prudence is also an important virtue to remember when giving advice to a friend. When prudence is lacking, words can cut to the heart and sting the people you love most. As Christians, we need to make sure the timing is right to share and ask our friend if she is even able to hear at the moment what we have to share. For this, prudence and timing work together!

As members of a busy and modern society, we need to be prudent with our relationships, especially on social media. When we are overwhelmed and upset, it might be easy to turn to Facebook, Twitter, or other social media accounts to vent. Social media is not a prudent place to post personal information that can ultimately damage relationships. Be prudent about what you say and how you say it as your words are powerful and can be misinterpreted and misread. Our screens can also isolate us when we overinvest in social media. Social media can be a tool for building relationships, but it doesn't replace spending time with others.

Another practical block in friendship related to prudence is being too impatient in our expectations of friendship, rushing the process of friendship or allowing relationships to die from lack of attention. We need to pace ourselves with our friendships, for some of us might come on too strong, and we need prudence to help us allow the friendship to grow at a healthy rate, slow and steady. A steady investment in relationships leads to healthy friendship.

No matter what changes you need to make in your life—whether they be taking time before acting, considering the consequences before speaking in person or on social media, or giving more or less attention to a friendship—Christ is there for you. When we Christians attempt to live smartly, we are able to see our lives from a new perspective. Your darkness might be like mine, needing to regroup, reassess, and make changes, while other people might need to stay on the path laid out for them and persevere. In either case, prudence will provide the roadmap. Prudence is the virtue that allows us to draw upon the truths of our Catholic faith and make choices that can help us when we are struggling.

Friendship in Progress: Developing and Deepening Friendships of Prudence

1. *Set realistic goals to develop and strengthen your friendships.* Prudence shows us how we should respond to

others and where we should invest our time, talent, and energy. It helps us evaluate which friends make sense for us to invest in at this point in our lives, especially when it comes to friendships that are centered on Christ. Call an old friend on her birthday, meet up in the evening with friends from Church, or make it your goal to develop some new friends who can support you in your Catholic faith.

2. *Pause before you share a word of criticism to others.* Allow the virtue of prudence to help safeguard your relationships and not allow them to be weakened and damaged by words. When we allow our passions, impulses, and stubbornness to lead our relationships, we end up in trouble. Criticism needs to be shared with love, and prudence is the virtue that shows us how to act in the moment.

3. *Be prudent when you post in the digital world on social media.* Prudence can safeguard not only our relationships but our reputations, especially online. For example, consider not posting pictures from an event until the day after to allow some time to pass as you decide what to share with all your friends on the Internet. Pausing before you hit post can protect you and your loved ones.

4. *Consider what talents to develop and use for God.* Prudence helps us be people of action. Prudence isn't simply about saying no; it can help us to be fully alive, as we learned in the life of St. Hildegard. What talents could you focus on developing and utilizing for God? How can prudence help you find the time you need to be your best version of yourself in your state in life? Prudence allows us to evaluate our gifts and talents and where to place our time and energy. St. Hildegard was able to develop a wide range of talents because she had a lifestyle that was

conducive to her development. What changes need
to be made for you to better glorify God?

5. *Pray for an increase in the virtue of prudence to help ourselves and our friends.* Ask the Holy Spirit to breathe
new vitality into your life and be prudent in your
undertakings.

Pray with us:

Come Holy Spirit, deepen the virtue of prudence in
my life.

Come Holy Spirit, show me how to be a prudent
friend.

Come Holy Spirit, bring me friends who exemplify
the virtue of prudence.

St. Hildegard of Bingen, Doctor of the Church, and
Bl. Jutta, pray for us.

5

Growing in Gratitude

St. Teresa of Avila and
Bl. Anne of St. Bartholomew

~Michele~

[Gratitude is a] thankful disposition of mind and
heart.

—"Gratitude," *Education in Virtue*

"What's on your plate today?" my husband asked me
at breakfast one morning.

"Ugh, I have to take Leah down to the genetics
clinic for her checkup," I complained. I hated going
down there. It was really annoying to have to go down-
town, pay to park, walk forever across a huge campus,
and then let all the doctors and nurses poke and prod at
my little one, who doesn't understand why she is even
there in the first place. "Why can't our kids be normal?"
I grumbled to my husband, knowing God was listening
as well. "Why do they get such weird things like genetic

disorders, eye cataracts, and extremely rare diseases like Guillain Barré?" I continued to complain throughout the morning as I talked to friends on the phone and then to God as I drove down the highway. "Sometimes you just ask too much of me," I told God. "Why can't you make things a little easier for me?"

As I unloaded the toddler and began walking the halls of the hospital, I passed many sick children along the way. Most of them had visible symptoms of illness or physical abnormalities. Many parents had panicked and rushed looks on their faces; some were even in tears. Doctors were explaining procedures and surgeries, nurses were shuffling patients to various departments, and all the waiting rooms I passed were full. My attitude quickly shifted, and I immediately thanked God for the blessing of four healthy children and the gift of good health care that was keeping my child from sickness. I was truly ashamed for all the complaining I did all morning, and I was overcome by a sense of gratitude as there I was with a healthy child.

As I got in the elevator, I was reminded of an experience that would stick in my mind forever, an opportunity to learn about gratitude from a friend who truly exemplified this virtue. Six years ago, when my son was hospitalized for paralysis due to a rare autoimmune disease, my friend Brenda had come to visit my son and me during the first few days of his hospitalization. We were all cramped into a tiny little room in the neurology department and had barely slept for days. She came right away, knowing the importance of friendship and support when someone is going through a trial, since her youngest had spent significant time in the hospital as an infant. As we talked, she shared how she praised God for that time in the hospital with her son, and in her gracious heart, she knew she was not there just for her son but also to pray for all the children who were there, especially those who had no one to pray for them.

I was completely overwhelmed at that thought. I wasn't angry, but I could barely string two sentences together in my mind at the time. How could I thank God for this opportunity and use it to pray for others? How could I break out of thinking about anyone else but my family and myself? However, as the days wore on and my son grew stronger, regaining his ability to walk, I started thanking God for each little step in his progress. I was also very grateful for all of my friends who were there for us during this trial. I began to spend less time worrying and more time praying for the sick children who surrounded us each day. By inspiring me to be grateful for the small blessings of each day, God prevented me from being closed in on my own little world and saved me from bitterness. I would have many more visits to the children's hospital in the years that followed, and this lesson of gratitude carried me through those visits.

My grateful friend continues to exemplify this virtue as her son is now battling leukemia. Over the years, as he has continued to undergo therapy, Brenda has shown an unbelievable attitude of gratitude. Not once have I ever heard her complain, ask why she had to endure this trial, or feel sorry for herself. In fact, the reports she would send out were full of praise to God and gratitude for everyone's friendship and support. Her posts were titled "Lord God, I Praise You for Your Compassion and Goodness" and "Taste and See the Goodness of the Lord." While they shared the details of the difficult journey, she ended every journal entry with, "We invoke prayers of gratitude every day for your love, prayers, and thoughtfulness." Even though her son had Down syndrome and leukemia, she boldly called him perfect.

Having friends of gratitude has been such a blessing in my life. Gratitude is an attractive virtue in others and can help us grow in our faith and develop meaningful and lasting relationships. Gratitude flows from humility, which, as St. Teresa of Avila shares, is the virtue that is most agreeable to God.[1] She writes, "If souls are humble, they will be moved to give thanks."[2] Gratitude helps us realize that nothing we have is earned but instead has come from God.

The first person we should express our gratitude to is God, because everything we have comes from him. St. Paul, in his many letters, exudes gratitude. We read in 1 Thessalonians, "In all circumstances give thanks, for this is the will of God for you in Christ Jesus" (5:18). In Philemon 1:4, he shares, "I give thanks to my God always, remembering you in my prayers," and in the letter to the Ephesians he writes, "I, too, hearing of your faith in the Lord Jesus and of your love for all the holy ones, do not cease giving thanks for you, remembering you in my prayers" (1:15–16).

Gratitude is one of the most beautiful virtues we can acquire. It makes our souls glow and helps us develop a generous spirit. The virtue of gratitude frees us from selfishness, isolation, and loneliness and helps us understand that we are made for each other and to live in community. When we are thankful for everything God has given us, we also receive consolation in times of difficulty, which helps us understand that God is with us, no matter the circumstances.[3] Pope Francis shared in an audience that gratitude "is a virtue that for believers is born from the same heart of their faith. . . . It is also the language of God, to whom above all we must express our gratitude."[4]

When we are thankful to God for all he has given us, our gratitude spills into our relationships. It helps cement bonds of friendship and shows the interior nature of the giver.[5] Alice von Hildebrand writes, "Gratitude is the blessed oil on which friendship and marriage thrive."[6] I think the world often underestimates the virtue of gratitude. I know I can forget how far a little thank you can go in making another person feel appreciated and loved, especially those with whom we are closest. Sometimes it is easier to be pleasant and grateful to the stranger holding the door open for us at the department store than to show gratitude to those with whom we spend a lot of time. We often take for granted all the acts of kindness that we experience from our friends.

As I pondered how important gratitude was in my friendships, I was reminded of a file I keep in my closet. It's full of thank-you cards friends have sent me over the years. They tell stories of gratitude for small acts of love that I have done throughout my life, such as sending Mass cards for the loss of loved ones, mentoring new nurses at work, praying for a friend's sick child, and holding the hands of many friends during the births of their children. My favorite ones are the letters simply thanking me for our friendship as these remind me just how important these relationships are to my life. One letter that especially stands out was an unexpected letter I received a few years ago from a grade-school friend. He wrote of an encounter more than twenty years ago. The sender had fallen away from the Church but was working at our parish as a custodian. I was practicing some music in the church basement one day, and we struck up a conversation. As he was about to leave, I asked if I would see him at Mass later. He confided he no longer went to church. I told him he was always welcome and left it at that. His letter, almost two decades later, thanked me for that small comment, one that would remain in his heart for several years until he was ready to accept it. It was a tiny, little seed that opened the door for him to step back into his faith, and now he has helped others return to the Church through the "Welcome Home Catholics" program. It was probably one of the best letters I've ever received. His gratitude for such a tiny, forgotten event filled my heart with joy.

Friendship of the Saints: Teresa of Avila and Anne of St. Bartholomew

"Reflect upon the providence and wisdom of God in all created things and praise Him in them all"[7] is one of the more familiar quotes penned by the famous mystic saint and Doctor of the Church Teresa of Jesus, often referred to as Teresa of Avila. A saint in the post-Reformation age, she lived during a difficult time for the Church and the world. Although she suffered greatly both physically and mentally, she praised God throughout her life. She was grateful for all that was given to her and reminded her sisters in the convent, "Do not be negligent about showing gratitude."[8]

St. Teresa was born in Spain in 1515. Her parents raised her to be devout and love God, inspiring her at a young age to be a nun. Her mother died in 1528, and her older sister, Maria de Cepeda, cared for her. Although Teresa was raised by virtuous parents and her sister also was a modest and good soul, she became friends with some of her cousins, who drew her away from her piety during this time. She wrote that these relationships changed her so much "that hardly any virtue remained to my naturally virtuous soul."[9] Teresa wrote that she learned an important lesson from these relationships with her cousins and wished she had instead had friends who taught her to fear God, which would have given her soul "strength not to fall."[10] Instead of caring what she looked like in the eyes of God, she worried more about her reputation. She began reading romantic tales and wanted to marry. After Teresa's sister Maria married, her father did not want her to live in a home without a "mother" and took her to be schooled and raised by the Augustinian nuns. There Teresa became friends with a nun of deep prayer, Dona Maria Briceno, whose holy ways influenced her. Once again, Teresa felt called to the religious life but struggled with her call. She became very ill and had to leave the school. While visiting her uncle, she was introduced to the *Letters of St. Jerome*, which helped her discern her vocation. After much prayer, she decided to enter the Order of Carmel at the Monastery of the Incarnation. She went against the wishes of her father, which pained her gravely. However, after Teresa's entry, her father had a change of heart.

After her profession, she became gravely ill and was paralyzed for three years. She slowly recovered, thanks to the intercession of St. Joseph; however, some residual effects remained. After the illness, she struggled greatly with prayer. But after eighteen years, she had a deep experience while reading St. Augustine's *Confessions*, felt deep contrition for her sins, and received the gift of tears.[11] She also began to experience supernatural occurrences in prayer. She had visions and revelations, but many people accused her of speaking with the devil and she was even taken to sit before the Inquisition, the judicial system of the Church then, whose goal was to fight heresy. She had a great desire to reform the Carmelite order, and in 1562 she founded the Convent of St. Joseph in Avila, the first reformed order of discalced

Carmelite nuns. She later started a reformed order for men and, with the help of St. John of the Cross, started a total of sixteen foundations for women and fourteen for men, which revitalized the Church during the aftermath of the Protestant Reformation.

Many men and women joined her in this mission. In 1572, a new lay sister professed into the convent of St. Joseph of Avila and took the name Sr. Anne of St. Bartholomew. She was a very holy woman, and St. Teresa made her prioress of the sick. From the moment Sr. Anne made her profession, she accompanied St. Teresa everywhere. Sr. Anne became St. Teresa's inseparable companion during her final fourteen years, during which St. Teresa experienced great illness and suffering. She became her nurse, secretary, and closest friend. With joy and gratitude, Sr. Anne cared for St. Teresa. She felt that she did not deserve the favor of living with a saint yet was grateful for the grace. Their friendship was marked with virtue, and Bl. Anne wrote in her autobiography, "Aside from the love I bore her and that she had for me, I had another great consolation in her company: almost continually I saw Jesus Christ in her soul and the manner in which He was united to it, as if it was his Heaven."[12]

Their friendship on earth ended in the most beautiful fashion. St. Teresa lay dying, no longer able to speak. Knowing how much Teresa appreciated cleanliness (because she was so pure, Teresa could not stand anything that was not clean[13]), Bl. Anne changed her linens and then helped Teresa into clean clothing. When she finished, St. Teresa was so pleased to have been cared for and to see herself clean that she looked at Bl. Anne "smilingly, and showed her gratitude by signs."[14] In the moments before St. Teresa died, Anne hastened to her side, and as the two saints embraced, Teresa rested her head in Anne's arms and her soul parted from her body.

Anne continued her friendship with Teresa after her death and prayed to her constantly. Teresa appeared to Anne one night and told her to ask for a favor and she would obtain it for her. Anne asked for the Spirit of God to always dwell in her soul. Anne continued the mission of St. Teresa and was the foundress of the Carmelites of Pontoise, Tours, and Antwerp. She was so well loved it was said that more than 20,000 mourners visited her body as it lay in state to touch it with religious articles for relics. Sr. Anne of St. Bartholomew was declared "Blessed" by Pope Benedict XV in 1917.[15]

St. Teresa's many writings were published after her death and are considered spiritual classics. They are practical guides to prayer and advancing in the spiritual life and have been read by many generations. She was given the title of Doctor of the Church in 1970, an honor previously granted only to men.

Obstacles to Gratitude

The story of St. Teresa dying in her friend's arms, her final gesture one of gratitude, is a very moving tale. How beautiful for Bl. Anne to remember that this amazing saint whom she had the privilege of befriending acknowledged her selfless service. Yet how often in our lives do we let acts of love and service go without mention? We live in a world full of ingratitude, and it has been this way throughout the ages. Jesus experienced ingratitude when he interacted with ten lepers. He healed all ten, yet only one returned to thank him. "Ten were cleansed, were they not?" he asked the one who returned (Lk 17:17). All had been given a new life and were freed from a terrible disease, yet only one gave thanks.

Gratitude can be difficult when we find ourselves blocked by sin. One of the biggest obstacles to gratefulness is comparison. Our friend St. Teresa of Avila writes, "Never compare one person with another: comparisons are odious."[16] As women, we constantly look at what everyone else has and wonder why we don't have that. We live in a world where everyone can flash their perfect new kitchens, cars, and families on filtered social media, and we begrudge what we don't have. St. Teresa is spot on: comparison is revolting. Instead of rejoicing in what has been given to our friends, we end up jealous, unhappy with and ungrateful for our gifts.

Envy is also a sin that can cause us to be ungrateful and can ruin friendships. Jealousy of what our friends have can poison our relationships. In this day and age, we can be especially prone to envy as we are constantly barraged with images of the perfect home, perfect children, and the "Pinterest-perfect life."

The solution to envy is gratitude. We will benefit from appreciating the gifts and qualities of our friends and being happy for their successes instead of feeling jealous. Pope Francis has shared how he overcomes jealousy: "When I am jealous, I must say to the Lord: 'Thank you, Lord, for you have given this to that person.'"[17] By breathing that prayer when we feel jealousy creeping in, we can avoid feeling envious.

When we are proud and think the world revolves around us, we also cannot be thankful. Our culture promotes an attitude of entitlement. We feel we are owed what we have and that we somehow earned it. In reality, we have not earned God's love and the blessings he has given us. We also aren't owed anything by our friends, nor do we deserve their friendship. We should be grateful for their presence in our lives and remember, with heaven as the goal of our friendships, "the gift of God is eternal life in Christ Jesus our Lord" (Rom 6:23).

Materialism also causes us to be ungrateful. The more we have, the more we want. In America, we are blessed to have abundance. Many people have a smartphone, a big-screen TV, two cars, and a beautiful home. Yet, as a nation, we are more ungrateful than ever. I remember seeing a video of a group of people who had gathered in Haiti after the terrible earthquake in 2010 in Port-au-Prince. This 7.0 quake had demolished what little they had in what was already one of the poorest countries in the world. Amid the death and destruction, thousands took the streets in a parade and sang "Praise the Lord" in gratitude that their lives had been spared; they showed the world that God is alive.[18] I was shocked at the response of gratitude, as many were left homeless and yet still thanked God. They were full of joy in their nothingness. Yet we live in a country with seemingly everything and for many there is no joy, no happiness, and no gratitude given to God.

Fr. Rocky, executive director of Relevant Radio, shares, "Gratitude naturally takes us away from ourselves and opens us to others and to God, and that always brings joy with it."[19] A recent study showed that people who are materialistic have a harder time being thankful for what they have and also are unhappier and more depressed than those who aren't materialistic.[20] Materialism is "me-centered" while gratitude is focused on others. When we realize everything we have comes from God and we did not earn it, we learn to be grateful; we are thankful to God and others, and we see that our days are filled with small acts of service and appreciate them more. This will bring us joy instead of unhappiness.

Another obstacle to gratefulness is when we refuse to forgive. When we do not forgive, we are being ungrateful to God for what he has done for us. God has forgiven us for every sin we have committed, and in gratitude we need to forgive others for when they hurt us. When we do not forgive, we become hard of heart and God's graces cannot enter in. We need to forgive our friends and free our hearts from the bondage that lack of forgiveness brings us.

Worry and anxiety can also lead us away from being grateful. When we are anxious, we lose our peace and forget to give thanks. Worry and anxiety create a vicious cycle. When we feel anxious, we worry instead of giving thanks and our thoughts become negative. Once we are in a dark or depressed mood, it is even harder to feel grateful. Although it is easier said than done, St. Paul reminds us in Philippians 4:6 to "have no anxiety at all" but instead encourages us to "let the peace of Christ control your hearts, the peace into which you were also called in one body. And be thankful. Let the word of Christ dwell in you richly, as in all wisdom you teach and admonish one another, singing psalms, hymns, and spiritual songs with gratitude in your hearts to God. And whatever you do, in word or in deed, do everything in the name of the Lord Jesus, giving thanks to God the Father through him" (Col 3:15–17).

Ungrateful people are difficult to be around; they are often chronic complainers, self-absorbed, jealous, and laden with unrealistic expectations of others. None of these are good qualities in a friend. We should all strive to be grateful to God and allow our thankfulness to flow into our relationships. Gratitude helps us appreciate our friendships and not take our friends for granted. When we are grateful, we are more deeply connected with our friends, and we look at our friendships honestly. It also encourages us to reach out more to our friends instead of being jealous. Pope Francis reminds us:

> If we can realize that everything is God's gift, how happy will our hearts be! Everything is his gift. He is our strength! Saying "thank you" is such an easy thing, and yet so hard! How often do we say "thank you" to one another in our families? . . . How often do we say "thank you" to those who help us, those close to us, those at our side throughout life? All too often we take everything for granted![21]

Friendship in Progress: Developing and Deepening Friendships of Gratitude

1. *Journal a list of your friends, and write why you are grateful for them.* Think about your friends and how they affect your life for the better. Write down all the things you're grateful for and the blessing each friend has been by being in your life. By purposefully calling to mind and reflecting on your friendships in this way, you'll be able to see the many gifts you have been given and thank God for your friends. It will also give you a sense of joy.

2. *Make a practice of writing thank-you letters to friends who have helped and supported you.* Receiving a note of thanks from a friend, especially when it is unexpected, can really make someone's day. Sharing how they have made a difference in your life can mean a lot to them and will strengthen your friendship.

3. *Host a Bible study on one of the letters of St. Paul with your friends to help you develop the virtue of gratitude together.* St. Paul writes constantly of his gratitude to God, praising and thanking him for the gift of his redemption. First and Second Thessalonians, First and Second Corinthians, Romans, Philemon,

Colossians, Ephesians, Philippians, and Second Timothy all discuss gratitude.

4. *Receive the Eucharist and attend eucharistic adoration with your friends.* Going to eucharistic adoration or Mass may be something you only consider doing by yourself, but going together as a small group can be a special time for friendship and strengthening your faith. The word *eucharist* means "thanksgiving." When we celebrate Mass, we remember how Christ gave his life for us on the Cross and we show our gratitude. Receiving Jesus' body, blood, soul, and divinity not only brings us joy but gives us the gift of his intimate presence. As we deepen our relationship with Jesus by spending time in prayer with him, we will grow in gratitude. St. Teresa reminds us after we have received him in Holy Communion we should spend time with Jesus. She wrote in *The Way of Perfection*, "Be with Him willingly; don't lose so good an occasion for conversing with Him as is the hour after having received Communion. If obedience should command something, Sisters, strive to leave your soul with the Lord."[22]

5. *Pray for an increase in the virtue of gratitude.* Thank God for everything he has given you, especially the gift of your friendships. Pray that we too can help our friends grow in this virtue.

   Pray with us:

   Come Holy Spirit, deepen the virtue of gratitude in my life.
   Come Holy Spirit, show me how to be a grateful friend.
   Come Holy Spirit, bring me friends who are grateful.
   St. Teresa of Avila and Bl. Anne of St. Bartholomew, pray for us.

6

Living Loyalty

Ruth and Naomi

~ Emily ~

[Loyalty is] accepting the bonds implicit in relationships and defending the virtues upheld by Church, family, and country.

—"Loyalty," *Education in Virtue*

The best indicator of a true friend is loyalty.[1] Scripture tells us, "A loyal friend is like a safe shelter; find one, and you have found a treasure" (Sir 6:14). We all desire to have friends who stand by us through thick or thin, who are unshakable and remain by our side during the good and the bad. Christian loyalty involves being honorable, trustworthy in our words and actions, and serving freely.

In my single days, I learned a life lesson about the meaning of the virtue of loyalty from my roommates,

Brooke and Jennifer Christine, known to her friends as JC. Through thick and thin, these friends were there for me and reminded me what it meant to be a friend. Their loyalty began with small acts of kindness, such as saving me a seat when we went out, including me in the evening plans, and picking up a coffee to encourage me to finish my late-night studies. However, their virtue of loyalty went deeper and was expressed in helping me uphold my morals and faith even in the midst of trials. My roommates would encourage me in my decisions so that not only my reputation but my moral code stayed intact. A true, loyal friend respects your free will but can still see your inner beauty and remains by your side when you fall. Even to this day, these friends continue to be a blessing in my life. As a matter of fact, these friendships have turned into two of the most important families in my children's lives, despite living a far distance away. I didn't realize at the time when I met my friends that Christ was giving me a treasure for not only myself but also my whole family in the years to come.

Our friendships have blossomed and matured over the years as we have passed through many different stages of life together. The three of us had distinctly different upbringings and personalities: JC was a "preppy" transfer student from a small, wealthy river town in Minnesota where she was raised boating with friends, playing sports, and spending time with her family. Brooke was a "crunchy" Vermont girl who loved nature, singing, and playing her guitar. Brooke's childhood was one of long hikes in the mountains and camping with her family. I was a "kid in khakis"—a perfect example of a suburban girl living in Ohio; I was driven by sports, always managed to have a boyfriend, and tried to master the game of life at a young age. Despite coming from three totally different backgrounds, we all shared the fact that we were from strong Catholic families. God knew that I needed to learn a few lessons on friendship from these special ladies, especially before I became a wife and mother.

One thing I knew when I met these girls was that I wanted to be a good friend. For the first time in my life, I wanted to choose solid female friendships over having a boyfriend. In my past, I was not always a good friend when I had a boyfriend; I would ditch my friends and allow my boyfriend to become the priority in my life. I wasn't always loyal to my friends, instead choosing short-term fun over the long-term investment of friendship. Looking back, I realize that I missed out on many wonderful memories by not choosing to be loyal to my female friends. If I could rewind time, I would prioritize my loyalties at a young age. I now see the importance of this virtue and how having good, loyal female friends journeying with me is a real blessing and an asset. My female friends offered me the potential for lasting friendships while my relationships with boys I dated would end with no future for friendship. I missed out on a lot of meaningful memories with my friends because I was exclusively hanging out with that one person rather than a group of friends.

My roommates witnessed to me the virtue of loyalty by their subtle and yet gentle ways of encouraging me to strive for holiness and stay loyal to the things in which I believed. They encouraged me to get up on Sunday morning and go to Mass, even after a late night out, and to have a healthy relationship with my boyfriend. Their faith in Christ was contagious, and through their loyalty to me I was able to witness how important it is to be true to your word and model the beliefs you hold through your own personal actions. These ladies would inspire me to not only grow in my Catholic faith but also reach out and share my gifts and talents with others. I noticed right away that they would stick up for me when I made silly mistakes and give me the benefit of the doubt when problems arose. It was refreshing to have such amazing women in my life teaching me about true friendship; slowly, I saw that I too was growing in my ability to be loyal to the things and people that mattered most to me. This in turn rekindled in me a desire to be a more faithful Catholic.

True charity grows loyal roots. It is easy to remain loyal to others when they are kind, loving, and thoughtful, but when you remain loyal when trouble hits, your loyalty proves to be sincere and Christ-centered. We all know that when you live with someone, you see all their shortcomings, and it's easy to become annoyed with them. When you have virtuous relationships, you can see past people's character flaws and imperfections. A loyal friend is supportive, respectful, trustworthy, and sincere. Christ used my roommates to help me grow in my understanding of these aspects of loyalty. They taught me how to be genuine and straightforward in my interactions and communication, and as a result, we actually got along better than I ever thought possible. At first, I was afraid of conflict and how it might ruin our relationships, yet slowly I learned that when you take the time out to communicate truth you are investing more in the friendship.

A loyal friend will speak truth with charity and remain your friend through thick and thin. Loyal friends don't give up on others, but rather, they hold out a helping hand and wait for the other person to reach out and grab it. For example, I always knew that my housemates had the best intentions despite any misunderstandings and difficulties that would emerge. Anyone who has ever had a roommate knows that troubles always arise;

disagreements, violations of personal space and property, and breakdowns in communication are inevitable. What made our arrangement unique was that my roommates and I were striving to be charitable like Christ, which made it easy to work things out in a way that always strengthened our friendships and deepened our bond of loyalty. It is easy to act cowardly and avoid difficult matters, but these ladies showed me that with good communication, "the truth will set you free" (Jn 8:32), and our friendships were deeper and more fulfilling as a result.

Having friends who would not tend towards gossip and betrayal was attractive and refreshing. A person who fulfills her duties in life proves to be a loyal friend. I knew that my roommates were trustworthy and had my back, and this knowledge strengthened my desire to become a more loyal person in all aspects of my life.

When we allow our spiritual friendships to be a great source of support, our friendships can become a catalyst for transformation as we go through life. Over the years, the friendship between Brooke, JC, and me has blossomed to include our spouses and children as well. What makes this triangle of friendship unique is that we go out of our way to support one another and nurture these friendships, despite distance and the busyness of life. Despite the fact that Brooke lives in Vermont, JC is raising her family in a small town in Ohio, and I live in the suburbs of Columbus, Ohio, we make it a yearly goal to get our families together and spend time doing activities that are fun and strengthen our faith. The more effort you put into your friendships, the more you are blessed, especially when you appear in a friend's life during difficult times. Over the years we have supported each other through child rearing, cancer, economic struggles, difficult pregnancies, depression, and despair. For example, I speak with Brooke every week for at least forty-five minutes on the phone so we can have a heart-to-heart conversation. My goal for the phone conversation is to be present to her and avoid the temptation to multitask.

A true friend knows that she is most needed when times get tough and reaches out to show support. Many people want to come to life's celebrations—the weddings and birthday parties—but how many of those same friends will come to your mother's funeral and remain loyal during cancer treatment, bankruptcy, or even a divorce? Loyal friends are there for you when you go through the good times and bad times. Being a loyal friend takes work and energy. We need to think outside of ourselves and realize that we are called not only to celebrate the good times but to console during the hard times. This is where spiritual friendship is strengthened, and the Lord can use these difficult times to help us turn to him for love and support.

Michele and I have learned this powerful lesson as we have worked side-by-side building a ministry, writing books, and speaking. The most important lesson we have learned is that we need to keep our eyes on Christ and know that he has blessed us with this opportunity to work together. Michele and I prioritize friendship over ministry and know that people are always more important than the task at hand. We have seen that when we desire to grow in loyalty and ask the Lord to help us grow in this area of our lives, our friendships will really flourish! This is true for everyone, not just us!

The Virtue of Loyalty

A loyal friend is consistent, faithful to her word, her people, her institution, and even her country. Loyal people are those of honor who understand what is important and worth defending in their lives. They are able to resist temptations, and the virtue of loyalty protects them when they are under personal scrutiny. "Loyalty engenders trust and preserves friendships."[2]

Looking at our lives through the eyes of our loyalties reveals a lot about our hearts. In life, we need to learn how to remain loyal to the people, places, and duties to which God has asked us to remain faithful. When we fulfill our Christian duties, we are better able to bear witness to the truth that Christ is always faithful to us. When we remain loyal to our spouses, family, dear friends, and employers, we exhibit stability.[3] A stable life is one that others take notice of and admire. A stable life means that we do not allow the winds and rains of our lives to bring us down. Loyalty and its companion stability are strong virtues to witness to others.

When we remain loyal in the little things, we are better able to remain loyal in the big things. Luke 16:10 states, "The person who is trustworthy in very small matters is also trustworthy in great ones; and the person who is dishonest in very small matters is also dishonest in great ones." Loyalty builds on loyalty. Christ wants us to be people of our word and display loyalty in our actions. In a complicated society, it is easy to lose a healthy perspective on what matters most, so we need to reaffirm our loyalties and follow through with faithfulness.

A gospel story that gives us much to reflect on is the interaction between Christ and his dear friend Peter right before the Crucifixion.[4] This exchange is heartbreaking and yet insightful in regard to how weak and vulnerable we can be without the help of the Holy Spirit to strengthen us in our ability to remain loyal and faithful to our friends as well as to our Lord and Savior:

After arresting him they led him away and took him
into the house of the high priest; Peter was following at a distance. They lit a fire in the middle of the
courtyard and sat around it, and Peter sat down with
them. When a maid saw him seated in the light, she
looked intently at him and said, "This man too was
with him." But he denied it saying, "Woman, I do
not know him." A short while later someone else saw
him and said, "You too are one of them"; but Peter
answered, "My friend, I am not." About an hour
later, still another insisted, "Assuredly, this man too
was with him, for he also is a Galilean." But Peter
said, "My friend, I do not know what you are talking
about." Just as he was saying this, the cock crowed,
and the Lord turned and looked at Peter; and Peter
remembered the word of the Lord, how he had said
to him, "Before the cock crows today, you will deny
me three times." He went out and began to weep
bitterly. (Lk 22:54–62)

One of the most striking aspects of this gospel passage is that Peter called the wrong people in the story
his friends. He called the people gathered around in
the courtyard, random strangers, his friends instead
of his Lord and Savior, whom he loved and pledged
his allegiance to just hours before Christ was taken
away. Peter got his loyalties confused when he took
his eyes off Christ was frightened by what other people thought of him. Sadly, in this passage, Peter never
made reference to Christ being his friend and denied
even knowing Christ—three times. Peter did not show
any remorse for his actions—not until the Lord turned
and mercifully gazed at Peter. Imagine the look Christ
gave Peter. Imagine how sad and disappointed he was
in Peter even though he knew and predicted this would
happen. After that penetrating look from the Lord, Peter
headed out and wept bitterly. However, just as Jesus

later forgave Peter for his denial, we too need to forgive and offer mercy to our friends for their shortcomings and denials. As Christians, we are called to be authentic in our friendships and allow these interactions to be a witness in a dark and confusing world.

Friendship of the Saints: Ruth and Naomi

One of the most beautiful stories in the Old Testament is the story of Ruth and Naomi. The book of Ruth shares their powerful story of friendship and reveals the godly virtue of loyalty and faithfulness even in difficult times. "Together the women weathered storms of grief, poverty, and desperation, and reached the happiest of ending."[5] Incredibly, this book of the Bible is named after the pagan Moabite woman who joined the Israelite people by her marriage and was interwoven into salvation history. This is a story that reveals that by being a loyal friend, we can impact others and lead them to Christ, resulting in a spiritual friendship that can even change the course of history.

The story begins in the time of the Judges (see Ruth 1:1), when God showed that the welfare of Israel depended greatly on the obedience or disobedience of the people to God's laws. Whenever the people of Israel rebelled or disobeyed, they were struck with famine, attacked by pagans, or struck by misfortunes that would lead the Israelites to repent and cause a great leader or judge to rise up to deliver them from hardship. In keeping with this theme, because of a great famine in Bethlehem, Naomi and her husband left the Promised Land and settled in the pagan country of Moab. Thereafter, her two sons married ungodly women, one of whom was Ruth, and within ten short years, her husband and sons died while her daughters-in-law remained barren. Naomi was so sick with desolation that she had her name changed to Mara, which means "bitter." Her life seemed pointless and broken.

Naomi felt so desperate that she advised her daughters-in-law to return to their former gods and ways of life while she returned to Bethlehem alone. One daughter-in-law listened and left, while Ruth, a Gentile, followed Naomi, a Jew, back to Bethlehem in search of a new life together. She had nothing but faith and was willing to remain loyal to the Lord, for Naomi's faith inspired Ruth to trust this new God, Yahweh, with her life. She turned her back on her former ways of life and headed towards the Promised Land. In Ruth 1:16–17, we read the words of Ruth to Naomi:

> Do not press me to go back and abandon you!
>> Wherever you go I will go,
>>> wherever you lodge I will lodge.
>> Your people shall be my people
>>> and your God, my God.
>> Where you die I will die,
>>> and there be buried.
> May the LORD do thus to me, and more, if even death separates me from you!

Once back in Canaan, Ruth meets Boaz, an influential landowner, and her virtues gain his attention. The relationship begins with him honoring her for how loyal she is to Naomi. He says, "I have had a complete account of what you have done for your mother-in-law after your husband's death; you have left your father and your mother and the land of your birth, and have come to a people whom previously you did not know. May the LORD reward what you have done!" (Ru 2:11–12). Ruth's yes to following Naomi and remaining loyal to her and her God allows her to be woven into salvation history. For Boaz declares his love for Ruth, and they marry and have a son named Obed who is to become the grandfather of King David. God shows us in this story that he always has a plan and that he richly blesses his loyal followers.

This story of loyalty and friendship from the book of Ruth is a great reminder of the impact we can have on others by being a faithful and spiritual friend. I think of how my roommates witnessed to me by their example and taught me about true friendship. I was able to learn about the virtues I wanted to develop based on their example as they witnessed to me in their daily life. We can come to appreciate and desire the virtues based on the behaviors of others in ordinary moments. I am certain that Ruth learned what it meant to follow Yahweh by Naomi's ability to remain faithful even when she was struck with such tragedies.

Obstacles to Loyalty

Nothing is more damaging to a friendship than disloyalty. Being trustworthy is a fundamental requirement for being a good friend. Sadly, when the people we love the most are not loyal, they can hurt us deeply with their intimate access to our own hearts. When we break our confidences in our friendships or others do so to us, we experience the violation of loyalty. When our fundamental ability to trust each other is missing, it affects how we view the world. Just look at how affairs lead to divorce and what these actions have done to spouses and their children. The breakdown in the family from affairs and disloyal behaviors has torn apart families, leaving Christ to pick up the pieces. God is loyal to us, and we are called to remain loyal to the people he has placed in our lives, especially those depending on us, such as our spouses and children. When we are disloyal and violate another's trust, we should turn to our Catholic faith for strength and help. Through the sacrament of Penance we can be forgiven and seek new graces for healing.

When others violate our trust, we need to remember that true charity sees the best in others and doesn't focus on the splinters and specks in our neighbor's eye. It is hard to remain loyal when you can't get past others' faults and you are always casting judgment.

In Matthew 7:1–5, Jesus states, "Stop judging, that you may not be judged. For as you judge, so will you be judged, and the measure with which you measure will be measured out to you. Why do you notice the splinter in your brother's eye, but do not perceive the wooden beam in your own eye? How can you say to your brother, 'Let me remove that splinter from your eye,' while the wooden beam is in your eye? You hypocrite, remove the wooden beam from your eye first; then you will see clearly to remove the splinter from your brother's eye." When we love others with Christian charity, support them, and refuse to cast judgment on them, we grow in the virtue of loyalty and strengthen our friendships.

A modern term that summarizes many friendships is *frenemy*, the concept of being a friend at one moment and the other person's worst enemy the next. This type of flipping and flopping between friend and enemy is rooted in disloyalty and immaturity. Done through whispers, slander, gossip, rumors, and hurtful humor, this type of "friendship" is downright disloyal.[6] Being a frenemy always hurts friendships and will never cultivate spiritual friendship.

However, like Peter, we usually don't expect to be disloyal. I recall a time I allowed my friendships to break down. I was young, and I was still learning how to balance a triangle of friends, similar to what Brooke and JC and I would be later. I was blessed to live in a neighborhood where my best friends lived within a block of my house. I spent countless hours playing with my friends, and yet the ageless question of "Who is your best friend?" always clouded our ability to get along as a threesome. Jealousy ruined many wonderful gatherings between the three of us.

I still recall the day the three of us were walking home from elementary school; the sun was shining, and it was a beautiful spring day, until, about halfway home, a simple argument over friendship turned into a cat fight. The three of us stood in a neighbor's front yard yelling over which of us were better friends with whom. Despite years of overnights, backyard fun, and countless hours on the phone, we were still fighting over friendship! Impulsively, I started to pull the hair of one of my friends and, with a wad of hair in my hand, yelled, "No, she is my friend, not yours!" I am happy to say that this was my one and only fistfight over friendship, but our friendship ended after this fight. This ridiculous battle is an example of how allowing sins against friendship can poison our relationships. It often has a lasting impact. If I only would have seen the role of remaining loyal to all my friends and wanting to protect my friendships, I am certain the outcome of our friendship would have been different. Friendship without loyalty is useless.

Friendship in Progress: Developing and Deepening Friendships of Loyalty

1. *Make a deliberate effort to defend your friends and acquaintances when others are speaking negatively against them.* These types of conversations can destroy your friend's reputation and break down the bonds of loyalty. It might be awkward and difficult

at first, but over time it will get easier to break the cycle of gossip.

2. *Find a spiritual mentor whom you can trust and go to for advice and counsel.* Ruth allowed Naomi to be her mentor and role model. Ruth was willing to follow her and take her advice because she was a trustworthy friend. Have you considered having a spiritual mentor or friend to help you in your life? Ask the Holy Spirit to send you mentors from whom you can seek out counsel or advice on important life matters. These mentors can be great people to bounce ideas off of and inspire you to grow in our faith.

3. *Evaluate your friendships in light of loyalty.* Do you have a pattern of broken friendships and relationships over the course of your life? Consider reconnecting with friends whom you have lost track of and try reaching out to them. Take baby steps into reentering the lives of friends and family members who have played a significant role in your upbringing and experience. Let these people know how grateful you are for their active role in your life.

4. *Develop a renewed attitude of loyalty to your friends, family, and community.* Focus on speaking in a positive tone and being grateful for the blessings you have received over the years. How can you show others your loyalty? Drop a quick note of appreciation in the mail, affirm others, focus on being prompt and prepared for events, and ask the Holy Spirit to show you how to live out this virtue in your life.

5. *Pray for the virtue of loyalty.* We can grow in loyalty by asking the Lord for assistance. Ask the Lord to help you be a better friend and be loyal to the people to whom Christ wants you to minister.

Pray with us:

Come Holy Spirit, deepen the virtue of loyalty in
my life.
Come Holy Spirit, show me how to be a loyal friend.
Come Holy Spirit, bring me loyal friends.
Ruth and Naomi, pray for us.

7

Giving Generosity

Sts. Catherine of Siena and Catherine of Sweden

~Michele~

[Generosity is] giving of oneself in a willing and
cheerful manner for the good of others.

—"Generosity," *Education in Virtue*

Ten years ago, my friend Christina called me and shared
the exciting news that she was starting a Catholic wom-
en's conference for our diocese. She and her Bible study
group felt called to take on this enormous task and were
looking for a few more volunteers to help fill the leadership roles. Since my husband had been attending Catholic men's conferences for years, I was delighted to hear
that something would be offered for women and immediately gave her my yes. Initially, I thought I would be
taking on a simple task, like helping serve bagels for

breakfast, but by the time I hung up the phone I found myself appointed secretary of the board of directors for the conference.

I would never have dreamed that this small little yes would change my life. With so many women giving of themselves freely for the Lord, not only was our first conference a huge success with a sell-out crowd of 1,000 women but through this process I learned about the virtue of generosity and was blessed by God with new friendships. When I walked into the first planning meeting, I had only been acquainted with a few women, but by the end of the process I'd made numerous amazing new friends, all of whom exemplified generosity and faith-filled living. Christina, our fearless leader, was a shining star of giving of herself to help others. As I watched her guide our team over the years and as our friendship grew, I often thought to myself that I could never give and sacrifice so much for others. She spent every second of her free time helping others. If she wasn't working on the conference, a full-time volunteer job, she was helping at her children's schools, making and bringing meals for friends who were sick, babysitting for a friend in need, or hosting fundraisers for Catholic organizations. She never counted the cost, complained, or was stingy. Instead she was generous and cheerful in her giving. Most importantly, she was generous with her time and her listening ear. She was always available to help a friend at a moment's notice. Her witness left a lasting impact on me and helped me reevaluate how I was using my life. Was I giving what God had given me as a gift to others? Was I generous to my friends?

I can see clearly now that God placed her in my life to teach me about the virtue of generosity. Generosity is a fruit of the Holy Spirit. It is a grace given by God to us. We live in a world that is fueled by selfishness, but as Catholics we are called to be generous as God is generous. He created us; he loves us and gave us his only Son Jesus to die on the Cross for us, the ultimate gift of generosity. If we look at Jesus' life, he spent his whole ministry healing, teaching, and giving to us, his friends; as he told us, "I no longer call you slaves, because a slave does not know what his master is doing. I have called you friends" (Jn 15:15). Jesus emptied his life out for our good, our salvation, and he continues to give us everything we need. We read in Ephesians that God has "blessed us in Christ with every spiritual blessing in the heavens, as he chose us in him, before the foundation of the world. . . . In love he destined us for adoption to himself through Jesus Christ" (Eph 1:3–10). God is so generous that he not only created us but also adopted us.

With God as our model, we too are to be generous to all those in our lives, especially our friends. Giving of ourselves is the highest gift we can offer another person. It is one of the best ways to show our love and friendship for others. Generosity stems from the virtue of love, and as we can never love too much, we can also never be too generous. When we are generous, we give of our time, our love, our patience, our attention, and our affection. God is never outdone in his generosity, so the generosity we show to friends is never too much. This is so important in friendship! Generosity opens our hearts up to grow deeper in friendship. Scripture tells us that "it is more blessed to give than to receive" (Acts 20:35). Being generous expands our hearts, refreshes our souls, and helps us to love more. When we are giving to others, we are filled with joy. No matter if our deeds are unappreciated or misunderstood, we should give our talents in the service of others. The more generous we are, the happier we will become.

God also blesses those who are generous with every grace. We read in 2 Corinthians: "Consider this: whoever sows sparingly will also reap sparingly, and whoever sows bountifully will also reap bountifully. Each must do as already determined, without sadness or compulsion, for God loves a cheerful giver. Moreover, God is able to make every grace abundant for you, so that in all things, always having all you need, you may have an abundance for every good work" (2 Cor 9:6–8).

I have personally experienced God's grace when I have given my time for him. One of my favorite stories to tell is when I was given a very special friendship because of my volunteer work with the conference and God blessed that friendship with an amazing gift. Just a little over a year after our first conference, I received an e-mail from a woman named Tobey who helped run another large Catholic women's conference about a speaker we were hosting that year. Since we both did the same type of volunteer work, we quickly became friends over the Internet through our e-mail conversations. We first shared only our conference ideas, but then our friendship began to deepen as we shared our lives. As we developed a strong relationship, we became more than pen pals, more like spiritual sisters. As our friendship grew, I had a strong desire to meet this wonderful woman who had become my friend, but with our busy lives and a long road trip between us, it just had never happened.

One Easter weekend, I returned to my hometown in Indiana and took my children to visit a large shrine that was next to our church, called The Shrine of Christ's Passion, to help them prepare for Easter. As it was Holy Saturday, the shrine was packed. We almost left since we could not even find a parking space, yet I was determined to spend at least a few minutes there, meditating on Christ's journey to Calvary. At the first statue we visited, there was another woman kneeling there, deep in prayer. My children were asking many questions, so I quickly whisked them away so as not to disturb her.

Just as we started walking toward the prayer trail, I saw a little boy running by. His shirt captured my attention as it listed his parish name and spelled out *Catholic* with symbols of our faith in place of letters. The image was unmistakable, and I recognized it immediately as one my friend Tobey had shared with me earlier this year. Knowing the parish was also where her children went to school, I asked the gentleman with the little boy if he knew a woman named Tobey who went to that parish. I will never forget his response. "She's right there," he said, pointing to the woman kneeling in prayer at the statue I had previously passed. I could hardly believe it! Neither of us knew the other was going to be traveling away from home that weekend. How was it that we were at the same destination, hundreds of miles away from our homes, at the exact same time? In addition, God sent a special clue so that we were able to recognize each other. I was completely overwhelmed with joy to meet my friend unexpectedly like this, but I knew it was a grace from God and a blessing to our work for him. One of my favorite quotations from St. John Paul II is, "In the designs of Providence, there are no mere coincidences." This was another example of his hand in my life. God is so generous that he even gives us gifts when we don't ask him for them, and he blesses our generous friendships.

Friendship of the Saints: Catherine of Siena and Catherine of Sweden

One year on our conference board of directors, three of us were named Michele (two of us spelling it "Michele" and one "Michelle"). Although it could be confusing sometimes for people to know which Michele to contact, I have always enjoyed having friends with the same name. This saint pair shares generosity and the same name of Catherine, which stems from the Greek word for *pure*.[1] These two amazing saints were influential holy women in the Middle Ages. They both gave of themselves willingly and cheerfully for the love of others in a way that was contagious and beneficial to the entire Church.

I have always been inspired by the life of the patron saint of nursing, the mystic and Doctor of the Church St. Catherine of Siena. Catherine was born in Italy in 1347 to Giacomo and Lapa Benicasa, the twenty-fourth of twenty-five children. She was a twin, but her twin sister, Giovanna, died in infancy, and Catherine was the favorite of her mother. Young and holy, she received a mystical vision of Jesus sitting on the throne of God when she was only six. Jesus smiled and gave her a blessing; it was a special grace she received, and from that point in her life, the "fire of Divine Love burned within her, enlightening her mind."[2] Catherine grew in virtue as a young girl, and everyone was amazed at her wisdom. At the young age of seven she made a vow never to marry and instead to become the bride of Christ. Although her parents tried very hard to find her a suitor, she did everything she could to avoid marriage. Her mother tried to get her to look beautiful, so at the advice of a holy friar, she cut off all her hair to make herself ugly. Her parents were furious at her attempts and made her live like a servant. They would not even let her have any time away by herself to pray. She instead learned how to have a space inside of herself where she could communicate with Jesus. Finally her father had a change of heart and told the family to allow her to do what Christ was asking her.

Catherine eventually joined the Third Order of St. Dominic. She belonged to a group called the Mantellate and wore the white tunic and black cape. These were not sisters but rather laywomen who lived in their own homes and cared for the sick and the poor. Catherine spent three years in deep prayer and then felt called to take her prayer to action. She first began her work with the poor, always being generous to those in the most need. Her biographer, Bl. Raymond of Capua, a close friend and Catherine's spiritual director, equated her generosity to that of St. Nicholas, who is known for his benevolence. Our tradition of gift-giving on Christmas stems from St. Nicholas. He also shares a story of Catherine's care for the poor. Once a beggar desperate for help approached her. Having nothing to give at the time but still wanting to help him, she broke off the cross of her rosary beads and gave it to the man. Later she had a vision of Jesus who showed her the cross, adorned with precious jewels. He told Catherine that because she gave the cross to him concealed as the beggar, he would "perfect her joy" and would return the cross on her judgment day before God so all could see her work of mercy.[3]

Another miraculous story was shared by Catherine's mother, who told of a time when Catherine began giving some of the family wine to the poor from a certain cask. Once opened, it should have lasted two weeks, but even with Catherine giving it away to the poor and their family drinking from the same cask, it continued to flow for months with the finest wine.

Catherine began giving more away, knowing it was a miracle. The wine flowed until the household servants decided to open the cask up to pour a new batch of wine inside, only to find that it was dry as a bone inside, even though they had just drank from it the night before.

Catherine's generosity also extended to victims of the plague. She worked tirelessly to care for them, sometimes sleeping less than thirty minutes a night. She nursed them in their sickness and buried them with her own two hands. She also visited those prisoners who were going to be executed, preparing them for their meeting with God. Catherine continued to give of herself and soon realized God was calling her to a greater mission, to become a peacemaker between feuding families and states. She even advised Pope Gregory VI and Pope Urban! She called for reform of the Church and kept many city-states loyal to the pope. She helped convince Pope Gregory to return from Avignon to Rome and helped establish peace between the government and the pope.

Toward the end of her life she was summoned to Rome. There she met and became friends with St. Catherine of Sweden, the daughter of St. Bridget of Sweden, foundress of the Bridgettines. Catherine of Sweden also gave of her life generously to others and the Church. She married young, but she and her husband took a vow of perpetual chastity. Catherine accompanied her mother when she moved to Rome and while there was widowed. There the mother-daughter team gave themselves to the work of God and created a hospice for Swedish students and pilgrims. Their work, along with Catherine of Siena's, was instrumental in convincing the pope to return to Rome from Avignon. When Bridget died in 1373, Catherine returned to Sweden with her mother's body, where she set up the religious order her mother had founded and directed it. Later, Catherine left Sweden and returned to Rome to help open the cause of canonization of her mother. It was at this time that she developed a deep friendship with St. Catherine of Siena.

During this time the Western Schism in the Church occurred, and two popes were elected, Pope Urban VI in Rome and the anti-pope Clement VII in Avignon. Both Catherines were strong supporters of the Roman papacy and even testified before a judicial commission in Pope Urban VI's favor. Both were highly commended by Pope Urban VI and were even asked by him to go on a mission together to speak with an immoral queen, Joanna of Naples. While the mission never materialized, their friendship is testimony that when God asks us to do big things, he will send us saintly friends to help us on the journey.

These two Catherines lived in a time of great upheaval in the world and the Church. There was great sickness, including the bubonic plague, and the tenuous state of the Church caused many people to lose their faith. They both gave their lives to help end the religious and political strife of the time. Their generosity stemmed from their great love of God and, as St. Catherine of Siena said on her deathbed to all those who followed her and accompanied her to Rome, "I shall be more use to you than I have ever been or could be while I was with you in this life. . . . Be certain of this, dearest children, that I have given my life for the Holy Church."[4]

Obstacles to Generosity

As we have seen from our saintly friends Catherine and Catherine, when we are generous with God and give for the good of others, he can work miracles!

However, being generous is not always easy. The big-gest obstacle to generosity is selfishness. Selfishness is when one only looks out for and promotes oneself and sometimes even puts oneself in the place of God. We all know selfishness doesn't need to be taught; it comes very easy to us due to original sin. No one wants a selfish friend, someone who always puts himself or herself first. Selfishness ruins relationships and leaves a bad taste in your mouth. St. John Paul II reminds us, "There is no place for selfishness."[5] We all have the ten-dency towards selfishness, and while there is give and take in every relationship, when we are unwilling to give to our friends and only take from them, it leads to imbalance. In our friendships, we need to be willing to go out of our way for our friends and put effort into the relationship. Developing true friendships means we have to give of ourselves and our time to the relation-ship and sometimes put others before our own desires. Selfishness binds us to think of only ourselves, but gen-erosity frees us to give ourselves to our friends without counting the cost. When we are generous and sacrifice for our friends, we are able to gain something for both parties: an investment in the friendship.

Another obstacle to generosity is stinginess, or being unwilling to give. We can be stingy in many ways, not giving our time, talent, or treasure. God did not cre-ate us to be closed-fisted or hard of heart. St. Catherine of Siena wrote in a prayer to God, "You, light, make the heart simple, not two-faced. You make it big, not stingy."[6] In the book of Sirach we read, "Before you die, be good to your friends; give them a share in what you possess" (Sir 14:13). One way to share what we have with our friends is to be hospitable. Hospitality is an important part of building up friendships, inviting our friends into our homes and sharing food, drink, and our

presence with our friends. I have noticed over my lifetime that my friends who are hospitable are surrounded
by many friends because they are always opening up
their homes in a generous manner to others. It is so
important that Pope Benedict XVI stated, "hospitality,
which [has] almost disappeared, . . . should be renewed
and enable people of all states of life to meet."[7]

As I look back on my life, I can think of times I have
been selfish or stingy in friendships, and I have always
regretted my behavior. The times when I see a number
on the caller ID and think, "I just don't have time for her
today" or "I can't handle hearing about her sad life or
asking me for one more thing." However, I will always
remember a time when the table was turned on me.
I had run into a friend who was visiting from out of
town and she offered to catch up for coffee with me on
the following day. Having recently moved to Columbus and not having any close friends in the area except
my husband at the time, I was looking forward to our
time together, which never materialized. Years later, we
were out together and ran into another old friend of
hers. When the opportunity to get together came up in
conversation, she said, "Yes, let's get coffee together."
After the friend walked away she told me, "That's my
standard line I say when people want to get together
and I don't want to." Remembering being ditched by
her a few years ago, I was stung!

If you have been burned by a friend who is selfish
or stingy, or who even has used you, that experience
may be an obstacle for you, causing you to be cautious
in your own generosity. However, we must remember
that just because we have been disappointed in one
friend's behavior, it doesn't mean that all friends are
like that. Also, while we are not called to be doormats
or allow others to take advantage of us, St. Catherine of

Siena reminds us we should be generous and not expect anything in return, even in the face of ingratitude. If you struggle with this idea, offer this prayer of St. Catherine:

> Eternal Goodness,
> You want me to gaze into you and see that you love
>   me
> To see that you love me gratuitously,
> So that I may love everyone with the very same love.
> You want me, then,
> To love and serve my neighbors gratuitously,
> By helping them
> Spiritually and materially
> As much as I can,
> Without any expectation of selfish profit or pleasure.
> Nor do you want me to hold back because of their
>   ingratitude or persecution.[8]

Friendship in Progress: Developing and Deepening Friendships of Generosity

1. *Be hospitable.* Invite your friends over for lunch, for coffee, or just to visit. Be generous in your hospitality of not only what you provide to eat or drink but also with your time and attention.

2. *Share your surplus with your friends.* Take some time out to evaluate what you have and what you can give away. By going through my closets once a year, I am often surprised at how many things are in good condition that I don't use. Offer your things to friends who could use them. For example, if your children have outgrown their clothes or you have gotten some new clothing, offer your gently used hand-me-downs to another friend. I have often been blessed with a surprise bag on my front porch containing clothing for my children; it always seems to arrive at just the time I need it.

3. *Evaluate how generous you are with your time to the Church.* Do you volunteer and give back to God? If so, what are your motives for giving? If not, think of one small way you can start sharing what God has given you. You may not be called to run a women's conference, but maybe you are called to help organize a small event at your parish or join an ongoing ministry there.

4. *Team up with a friend to give generously to others.* If you are overwhelmed with life and feel like you can't always give, Emily and I have found a simple solution. We like to call it finding a "mercy partner." Emily and I often work together doing acts of mercy when friends need our help. For example, if bringing an entire meal is too difficult or expensive, we can each provide part of the meal or go in on a gift card, or one of us will babysit the other's children so the other can visit a friend in need.

5. *Pray for an increase in the virtue of generosity for yourself and for your friends.* Ask God to soften your heart and help you be willing to give, even if it means a sacrifice.

Pray with us:

Come Holy Spirit, deepen the virtue of generosity in me.

Come Holy Spirit, show me how to be a generous friend.

Come Holy Spirit, bring me friends who serve you generously.

Sts. Catherine of Siena and Catherine of Sweden, pray for us.

8

Pondering Prayerfulness

Mary, Mother of God, and St. Elizabeth

~ Emily ~

[Prayer is having a] personal relationship with the living and true God. . . . "Prayer is the raising of one's mind and heart to God or the requesting of good things from God."

—*Catechism of the Catholic Church*, 2558–2559

"Emily, you can't afford not to pray," my brother, Fr. Jonathan, told me one day. These few words cut through my foggy haze of motherhood like a strong cup of coffee. All of a sudden, it made sense to me; I realized I was not praying except for going to Mass on Sunday, before meals, bedtime prayers, and the occasional "Please help me, God!" aspiration. For many years, my main goal of the day was surviving motherhood, which was a vortex that sucked all my time, attention, and energy. In a few short years my life had been flipped upside down. The rapid transition from a happy, single woman to a happy, married woman with three children under the age of four left me spinning. I knew I was guilty of neglecting regular prayer, and I felt that motherhood was holding me back from growing spiritually. I was always waiting for a quiet time to pray instead of allowing my contemplation to take place in union with my vocation.

I knew I needed some expert advice, but instead of turning to my Catholic faith for counsel, I turned to secular sources for strength and assistance. I realized quickly that this was not enough. I needed to not only be a good mother but to develop a prayer life that could help me in my new life. St. Augustine shares with us in his *Confessions*, "my heart is restless until it rests in you."[1] I knew that what I needed was a relationship with God and that I needed to develop the virtue of prayerfulness to help me in my life.

One friend who has guided me in learning the virtue of prayerfulness is my friend Emily. I met her on Martin Luther King Jr. Day about six months before I got married, during a casual conversation at the Catholic bookstore at my college. The encounter blossomed into a friendship that would expand to our other family members and deepen over the years. Although Emily is six years younger than me, this joyful young woman would become one of my dearest friends, and we are still very close to this day.

Emily has always been a prayerful woman. Not only does she have a deep prayer life herself but she also has taught me how to pray. Through the intimate bond of prayer in our friendship, our relationship has grown in a way I could never have imagined. Emily's deep prayer life stems from a love of souls. She desires heaven for everyone and that love for others motivates her to be a woman of prayer. She is also a living testimony that through great loss comes lifelong graces and blessings when you are a person of faith. Tragically, she lost her older brother to cancer while he was a teenager. Daniel's passing shed great spiritual light into her soul, affirmed for her that God was real, and sparked a great desire to see her brother in heaven someday. Her daily mission is to love God and serve him no matter what life tosses at her.

Emily doesn't just walk the walk and talk the talk; she really prays the prayers! Emily is entering her final year of a seven-year discernment to become a member of the Lay Carmelite Order (Definitively Professed Discalced Carmelite). Although she is the youngest member in the Columbus chapter, she has formed deep spiritual friendships through monthly meetings and special celebrations for Carmelite feast days. Her commitments include praying the Morning and Evening Divine Office, a daily Marian devotion, thirty minutes of mental prayer, daily examination of conscience, and monthly Confession. She has taken time out of her busy life to develop her prayer life and cultivate spiritual gifts that she uses to bless others. She has taught me to seek these gifts from the Lord like a young child begging for special gifts at Christmas time. My friend pleads with the Lord for the virtues and gifts that will help her and her family grow in holiness. She begs the Lord to help her grow in patience, humility, peace, joy, wisdom, and fortitude. She knows that spiritual gifts far outweigh the things of this world and asks for these gifts to be bestowed on her family and friends.

Each year Emily's favorite birthday gift is the chance her family gives her to go on a silent retreat for time to pray and meditate. As a busy mother of five, she must be tempted to head to a day spa, go on a girls' weekend, or reward herself with a shopping trip, but instead she chooses to get her spiritual house in order. This yearly retreat allows her to step away from the busyness of life and refocus her eyes on Christ and her eternal destiny.

Emily has also taught me the invaluable lesson of uniting my prayer with my daily work. Once while I was visiting her, she was cleaning up the dishes from breakfast and asked, "Will you pray with me?" As soon as I said yes, she hit a button on her smartphone and the Divine Office started to play. We quietly cleaned up after the young children while saying the whole Office of Prayers. I left her house inspired and amazed at how this mother was committed to prayer despite having young children, a career, and a busy life.

Emily also involves prayer in other parts of her life. I recall going on runs with her when she would encourage me to offer up each mile for a friend in need, or we would say a decade of the Rosary out loud while we were jogging. The scriptures are always on her tongue as a source of strength and hope during her trials, and she is quick to remind me of these sacred words in friendly conversation. She makes Christ's words come alive as she relates them to everyday moments.

As a spiritual friend, she is always there to pray with me and support me in my journey. I recall one particular moment when I was having a difficult day and called her for support. My intention of the phone call was to vent about someone and a difficult situation in my life. However, because Emily is a prayerful friend, she invited me to pray with her right then and there. By the time I hung up the phone I not only felt better but the time spent in prayer had also renewed my spirit. The feelings of bitterness and resentment passed, and I was able to let go and let God deal with the matter.

Through Emily, I now realize that when it comes to prayer, we shouldn't just wait for life to slow down enough to begin. In fact, it is precisely when things are at their busiest that we need to pause and pray. Prayer is our lifeline, our way to communicate with God. Through conversation with him, we receive not only encouragement but also graces that will help us in our daily lives. Often, we are tempted to trade in our silence and prayer time for the business of doing and going; we then wonder why we are burned out and struggling through our days. It is because we have not taken the time to rest through prayer.

Echoing my brother's advice, Emily has shown me that life is too important not to pray. The more we develop a balanced prayer life of meditation, petition, intercession, praise, and worship, the better women of God we will become. With our minds set on heaven, instead of earthly goals, our lives take on new meaning. Developing the virtue of prayerfulness not only helped me in my personal growth and journey to God but I have also come to learn the gift of praying for others is one that is far greater than gold. Prayer not only feeds our souls but also strengthens others.

The Virtue of Prayerfulness

Prayerfulness is the calling for us to interact with God our Creator on a personal and intimate level (see *CCC*, 2700–2724). Prayer activates the heart and teaches it to engage with the spiritual world where we reach out to the Holy Trinity, the saints, the Blessed Mother, and the holy angels for strength to grow in holiness. You cannot be a Christian without the virtue of prayerfulness.

Prayerfulness is necessary to practice all the virtues and grow in holiness. St. Ephrem of Syria tells us, "Virtues are formed by prayer. Prayer preserves self-control. Prayer suppresses anger. Prayer prevents emotions of pride and envy. Prayer draws into the soul the Holy Spirit, and raises man and woman to Heaven."[2] In the biography of St. Catherine of Siena, Bl. Raymond of Capua writes, "she practiced prayer and made it a continual habit as she had realized that it strengthened and increased the other virtues, whereas without it they weakened and withered away."[3]

When we have God at the center of our lives, we can be better friends. Prayerfulness is a virtue worth developing and cultivating no matter our age or stage in life, and it is one we should share with our friends. I have found that when I take the time to pray, God always rewards me for slowing down and honoring him. Just as Christ taught his disciples how to pray, we too need to have spiritual friends whom we can pray with, learn from, and be inspired by as we walk the path to holiness. Friends can make a difference when they inspire us to holiness, by nudging us toward God.

Praying together also builds bonds of loyalty and love. We help our friends achieve personal goals; therefore we should also be willing to help them grow spiritually.

The Catholic Church helps us on our path to holiness and even offers us actual grace for this epic journey toward heaven. She cares for us with the holy sacraments; we start the journey with Baptism; we are fed with the Eucharist, our heavenly food and nourishment; we are forgiven through Penance; we are healed with the Anointing of the Sick; we are strengthened with

Confirmation; and with much celebration and joy, we are launched in our vocations with Holy Orders or Matrimony. Yet without prayer, we can lose our way, fall into temptations, and drift apart from our Lord and his Church. Prayer strengthens us for the journey, and friends sweeten our life as we head toward heaven.

Friendship of the Saints: Mary and Elizabeth

Mary, the mother of Jesus, is the queen of heaven and earth and the ultimate role model of prayerfulness. As a young Jewish girl, she was raised with the anticipation and hope of the Messiah's arrival and learned to pray and read the Torah.

In the Gospel of Luke, we learn about a beautiful encounter between the Blessed Mother and her cousin Elizabeth. Beginning in Luke 1:36, the angel Gabriel tells Mary that her cousin Elizabeth, who was advanced in age and had not been able to bear a child, was expecting. The angel Gabriel shares this message with Mary as a sign meant to assure her. He ends his meeting with Mary with the words that we should all reflect upon: "For nothing will be impossible for God" (Lk 1:37). After hearing Gabriel's message, Mary proclaims the powerful words, "Behold, I am the handmaid of the Lord. May it be done to me according to your word" (Lk 1:38).

Imagine the joy Mary experienced when she heard the news that her cousin, Elizabeth, who was without child, was pregnant, would become the mother of the great and final prophet, John the Baptist—the voice crying out in the desert, making way for the Lord, his cousin. Her first action after the annunciation was one of service and love as she went with haste to the hill country of Judah to serve Elizabeth.[4]

When Mary arrived in Judah, a difficult journey of about three days from Nazareth, she was greeted by Elizabeth's bold salutation. Elizabeth, filled with the Holy Spirit, proclaimed the powerful words, "Most blessed are you among women, and blessed is the fruit of your womb! And why is this granted me, that the mother of my Lord should come to me?" (Lk 1:42). Although Elizabeth had not received a visit from an angel like her husband had, she was a prayerful woman and knew Mary was carrying the Messiah through the prophetic insight of the Holy Spirit. These words given to us by Elizabeth in scripture are the exact words we recite over and over again while saying the Hail Mary.

The women continued this prayerful encounter as Mary responds in humility with the Magnificat: "My soul proclaims the greatness of the Lord; my spirit rejoices in God my savior" (Lk 1:46–47). Scripture does not reveal much more about this encounter, but we do know that Mary stayed with Elizabeth for three full months. They would spend their days cooking, cleaning, and as two devout Jewish women, praying the psalms together as Mary served Elizabeth throughout her final trimester. What a beautiful gift Mary gave of herself in service and prayer! The two pregnant women were "now intimately bound through their experience of miraculous motherhood and the children they bear."[5]

The Blessed Mother was the first evangelist in the New Testament. She brought Christ, still in the womb, to Elizabeth and her unborn child to proclaim the Good News. This holy and prayerful encounter gives us a glimpse of Mary's role not only in the life of her cousin Elizabeth but also in the whole Church for generations to come. Mary and Elizabeth gave themselves completely to God's divine plan and from it bore our salvation. Mary is also willing to come to us and bring us to Jesus, wherever we are in life. She desires that we know her son and love him as she does, for "Mary magnifies Christ."[6]

As I reflect on my own life, I realize how the Visitation of Mary has been a great source of consolation and renewal in my life. In 2000, I was three months pregnant with my second child when I went on a jubilee trip to the Holy Land. As I walked the same streets where Mary met Elizabeth and as I prayed in the Church of the Visitation, I was in awe over how much I needed Mary in my life. Mary showed me the way, brought me to Christ, and was the mother I desired to be. I was pregnant with my second son, who was going to be born only fifteen months after my oldest child, and my husband was back in school for a second degree; we were broke, and yet this trip fell into our laps as a gift. As I knelt there, my prayers consisted of pleas that God would help our family, that he would make me a strong woman able to trust him with my life and open to his plans for my life, just like Mary was open to the Holy Spirit.

Years later, I was gifted with my own visitation experience, right here in my hometown, when Michele and I were both pregnant at the same time. Early in our pregnancies, we learned we were due within three weeks of each other. Although this was my sixth pregnancy and Michele's third, we had never had children in the same year. What a joy it was to celebrate this wonderful gift of new life with a dear friend! This experience added another layer to our friendship, a special mother-to-mother bond, as we were able to compare our pregnancies and talk about the new lives growing within us. Like Mary and Elizabeth's relationship, God used this special time to prepare us for something we could never have imagined, that some day, we would birth a ministry together that strengthens women in their faith life and proclaims the Gospel.

Our story gets better. On June 8, 2011, Michele was induced three weeks early for some medical complications and delivered Juliana Rose at 3:52 a.m. Amazingly, I went into spontaneous labor and delivered Mary Therese at 4:59 a.m.—we gave birth a little over an hour apart, just a few rooms over in the same hospital! No one could believe it. We were the talk of the nurse's station. Even the housekeeping staff was talking about it! Our first visitor, my brother, Fr. Jonathan, came a few hours after the babies were born. He arrived before beginning his priestly duties for the day to come and bless the babies. Michele then called the hospital chaplain and asked that Holy Communion be brought to our rooms. We gathered in that little hospital room, shared the Word of God with the eucharistic minister, and received the gift of Jesus in the Eucharist. It was a powerful witness to the beauty of prayerfulness in friendship! I believe God blessed us with this shared memory to affirm that we need to trust in his ways and desire deeper spiritual friendships.

When we choose to allow other women into our lives and develop spiritual friendships, we are blessed beyond our imagination. When we are willing to develop a prayer life and engage in this prayer life with our spiritual friends, like Elizabeth and Mary, we are given a gift for all of eternity. What a gift it must have been for both women to have this prayerful friendship and to have each other as a source of strength as they partook in God's divine plan for salvation history! The relationship of the Blessed Mother and Elizabeth is an example of the type of friendship we are all called to have. When we combine prayer with service to others, we are able to be the heart and hands of Jesus Christ.

Obstacles to Prayerfulness

When looking to grow in prayerfulness, we need to evaluate what obstacles hold us back. Spiritual friendships cannot happen unless we are open to having a relationship with God in prayer. Some of the most common obstacles to growing in our own prayer lives are being distracted in our prayers, experiencing dryness, questioning our faith, encountering spiritual sloth, and being too busy to pray. These struggles are natural and yet challenging. When we find ourselves struggling, we need to remember that Christ is there for us to help us work through these challenges. Prayer needs to be what feeds our good works and action throughout our lives so we can discern what Christ is calling us to do. Prayer is not an option; it is necessary for Christians who seek to renew the Church.

The second set of obstacles relate to friendship and prayerfulness. Establishing spiritual friends and starting spiritual friendships can be challenging. Being a friend of prayer can help form deep and lasting relationships, but starting these types of friendships can be intimidating and difficult.

The first thing we need to do is begin praying for our friends in our lives. I have many friends for whom I have been praying for more than twenty years, but they don't even know it. It is important to cover our friends in prayer and see how God wants to use these friendships to glorify him. The great thing about covering our friends in prayers is that we have an extra-special bond with them of which they are unaware.

The second thing we can do is to pray with our friends as much as possible. For example, when I called my friend Emily after a long and difficult day, she replied with, "Let's pray about this right now." It might seem strange at first, but including Christ in these difficult or joyful moments will only strengthen your friendship. It doesn't have to be for a long period of time. Emily calls it "The Holy 5," meaning we would pray for just five minutes. Philippians 4:6 states, "Have no anxiety at all, but in everything, by prayer and petition, with thanksgiving, make your requests known to God." We are called to make our requests to God and remember that no problem is too large or small for Christ.

The third step for establishing prayerfulness in friendships is to remember to always extend a helping hand; just as the Blessed Mother came to Elizabeth to serve her during her pregnancy, we need to do the same. We need to not just talk about being compassionate and serving others; we also need to act without expecting anything in return. We must remember to always be a friend first by caring and being involved in each other's lives and then by establishing spiritual friendships just like our Lord did: he first found his disciples and then taught them to pray. St. Gregory shares with us, "We are linked by the power of prayer, we, as it were, hold each other's hand as we walk side by side along a slippery path; and thus by the bounteous disposition of charity, it comes about that the harder each one leans on the other, the more firmly we are riveted together in brotherly love."[7] It is essential to meet people where they are in life and know that with prayer we are able to help others.

For example, Michele and I had a mutual friend, Liz, who was battling breast cancer, so we organized a group party for her. Inspired by our friend Stacey, we hosted a "Loving Liz" party at my parents' house to shower her with support. We invited all her friends, people from many stages of her life, and showered her with gifts. It was such a joyful night as we sat around the pool in the backyard, making new friends and rekindling old friendships. Toward the end of the night, we headed inside and had a short prayer gathering. We prayed for Liz with all our hearts and extended our hands over her in prayer, asking Jesus to be with her during this harrowing journey and heal her. Many of our mutual friends had never experienced this type of prayer and later told us it was a turning point in their own spiritual lives. That night, we sent everyone home with a rosary bracelet to remember to pray for Liz every day, just like we had done for Stacey years before. Although we could not always be physically united with our friend, we wanted her to know that we were praying for her, especially during her difficult moments.

The key to developing spiritual friendships is to allow the Holy Spirit to show you the path he has laid out and the people whose lives he wants you to touch. When we allow others into our prayer life and cultivate spiritual friendship, we gain spiritual insights. Close spiritual friends often provide us key insights, helping us navigate the spiritual life and the many decisions that directly impact our lives. We all experience difficulties in our own prayer lives, but as friends, we can inspire each other to work through these challenging times and pray with our friends in order to provide them support.

In closing, let us remember these powerful words from the Gospel of Matthew: "Again, [amen,] I say to you, if two of you agree on earth about anything for which they are to pray, it shall be granted to them by my heavenly Father. For where two or three are gathered together in my name, there am I in the midst of them" (Mt 18:19–20).

Friendship in Progress: Developing
and Deepening Friendships of Prayerfulness

1. *Pray for your friends by name.* Make a list of your friends in a journal, or you can even download a prayer app like Echo Prayer Manager. Put your friends' names on the list to remind yourself to pray for them. Another idea is to jot down names of your friends on your day calendar, so you remember to pray for them throughout the entire day.

2. *Spend five to ten minutes a day in prayer.* Create a sacred space in your home where you feel comfortable praying. Schedule the time on your calendar, and keep it like you would any other appointment. This is the key to developing a relationship with God, which is necessary before we can develop spiritual friendships. We cannot know what God wants from us without developing a real and personal prayer life. It is akin to seeking out a friendship with someone but remain unwilling to communicate at all: no calling, texting, or messaging—and yet wonder why we are not close! Prayer is the key to getting to know God better and allowing the Holy Spirit to help us develop lasting and healthy friendships.

3. *Find a friend with whom you can begin to pray; if you don't have someone to pray with, ask God to give you this special friend in your life.* As I mentioned, this can be uncomfortable at first, as prayer is very intimate. You can start by meeting for Mass or saying memorized prayers together, such as a decade of the Rosary or the Chaplet of Divine Mercy.

4. *Start or join an exercise prayer group.* There is a growing trend to blend fitness with the Catholic faith. Many churches host Pietra Fitness and Soul Core workout programs. If you don't have these programs, you can meet up at a park and walk or run

together while praying the Rosary, the Chaplet of Divine Mercy, or other devotional prayers.

5. *Pray for an increase in the virtue of prayerfulness for yourself and for your friends.*

    Pray with us:

Come Holy Spirit, deepen the virtue of prayerfulness in me.

Come Holy Spirit, show me how to be a prayerful friend.

Come Holy Spirit, bring me friends who pray.

Holy Mary, Mother of God, and St. Elizabeth, pray for us.

Appendix 1

Prayers

St. Matilda and St. Gertrude, pray for us.

St. Perpetua and St. Felicity, pray for us.

St. Thérèse of Lisieux and Servant of God Léonie Martin, pray for us.

St. Hildegard of Bingen and Bl. Jutta, pray for us.

St. Teresa of Avila and Bl. Anne of St. Bartholomew, pray for us.

Ruth and Naomi, pray for us.

St. Catherine of Siena and St. Catherine of Sweden, pray for us.

Mary, Mother of God, and St. Elizabeth, pray for us.

St. Francis and St. Clare of Assisi, pray for us.

St. Augustine and St. Jerome, pray for us.

St. Francis de Sales and St. Jane de Chantal, pray for us.

St. Louis Martin and St. Zélie Martin, pray for us.

St. Basil the Great and St. Gregory Nazianzen, pray for us.

St. John Paul II and St. Teresa of Calcutta, pray for us.

St. Philip Neri and St. Ignatius, pray for us.

St. Martin de Porres and St. Rose of Lima, pray for us.

St. John Bosco and St. Dominic Savio, pray for us.

St. Faustina and Bl. Fr. Sopocko, pray for us.

St. Cosmas and St. Damian, pray for us.

St. Patrick and St. Brigid of Ireland, pray for us.
St. Benedict and St. Scholastica, pray for us.
St. Augustine and St. Monica, pray for us.
St. Peter and St. Paul, pray for us.
St. Anne and St. Joachim, pray for us.
St. Adrian and St. Natalia, pray for us.
St. James and St. John, pray for us.
St. Catherine of Sweden and St. Bridget of Sweden, pray
   for us.
St. Pio of Pietrelcina and St. John Paul II, pray for us.

Prayer of St. Gertrude for Our Friends (adapted)

O most kind and gentle Jesus, I commend all those who have asked my unworthy prayers to your divine knowledge and love. In union with that love through which you commended your Spirit to the Father, I commend them all to your Sacred Heart and ask you to enclose them within it. I offer and set these prayers before you, in union with the love with which you took a true human heart for the salvation of the whole human race and gave it as a token of your special friendship to your well-loved friends. I beg you to take from your infinite treasures and bless all those whom I pray for and am bound to pray for.

O good Jesus, I offer you this prayer to your everlasting praise, and through it, I ask that you send many benefits and blessings to those who are dear to you and to me, according to the good pleasure of your divine compassion.

Prayer to St. John the Apostle, Patron Saint of Friendship

St. John, Glorious Apostle and much-loved disciple of Jesus, you were a faithful friend to Christ and stayed by his side through his Passion, Death, and Resurrection. Help me to be a good friend to others, and bring my friends close to the heart of Jesus.

Please beg before the throne of God that I may be a friend of faith, hope, love, prudence, gratitude, loyalty, generosity, and prayerfulness and that friendships of virtue come into my life.

St. John, please intercede before the throne of God that I may be blessed with faith-filled friendships that continue into eternity. Amen.

Prayer for Forgiveness in Friendship

Dear Lord, I ask you to mend the rift between my friend (*name*) and me. Help me to offer my sincere apology for anything I have said or done to hurt my friend and extend forgiveness for anything she has done to offend me. I ask you to bless my friend and to give her all she needs to be happy and fulfilled. I thank you, Lord, for helping us work through our wound and for healing us. Thank you for using this opportunity to help sanctify me. I praise you Lord and give this wound to you. Please heal our relationship. May your perfect plan lead us to complete joy. Amen.

Study Guide

We are so glad you have decided to dive deeper into *The Friendship Project* by joining a group study! As we can attest, small faith-sharing groups have introduced us to many wonderful new friends and deepened other friendships in both of our lives. Whether you are doing this with two or three girlfriends in your living room or a whole room of women at your parish, we know you will be blessed with new and strengthened relationships. Please know we are praying for you as you journey towards deeper and lasting friendships.

Instructions for Facilitators

We have written this study to be conducted in eight one- to two-hour sessions, but feel free to use a timetable that works best for your group. You may also wish to add an introductory session for passing out books, making introductions, pointing out special features and downloads on the website, and discussing the introductory questions provided in the study guide below.

Begin each session by watching a short video available for free at www.thefriendshipprojectbook.com. Each video includes new, complementary teachings not included in the book as well as a chance to get to know us, the authors, and meet our friends whom we've written about in this book through unique interviews. Study questions are provided for group discussion and are designed to help the participant process and implement many of the concepts presented throughout the book. Each session also includes a Going Deeper into Scripture section, which allows the group to ponder a scripture verse from each chapter and meditate over God's word together. At the end of each session, we invite your group to offer their prayer intentions and pray together the original prayers offered at the end of each section. These prayers are written to help us grow in each virtue and to see these virtues implemented in our friendships.

We always tell group leaders that there are no right or wrong ways to use this study. We will offer some suggestions below to help you get started, and please know we are always available for questions on our website and social media platforms.

MATERIALS NEEDED

- *The Friendship Project* book
- Internet access to stream the free videos for each chapter found at thefriendshipprojectbook.com. If you can't stream the videos, you can purchase a DVD on our website.
- Optional: Download the free journal found at thefriendshipprojectbook.com.
- Optional: Download the free "bonus" material sheets including the "Friendship in Progress: Deepening and Developing Friendships" handouts and other materials available to help strengthen faith-filled friendships on thefriendshipprojectbook. com.

- Optional: Sign up for our e-mails and follow us on social media to connect with us.

HOW TO GET STARTED

- *Watch the facilitator video at thefriendshipprojectbook. com.* Visit us online for more instructions on how to lead a group. We encourage you to sign up for our e-mail list for important updates and blog posts from us.
- *Decide where and when the group will meet.* Whether in your home, a coffee shop, or in a room at your parish—in the morning, afternoon, or evening— find a place, day, and time that works best for your group.
- *Promote your study group.* Invite your friends, place an announcement in your church bulletin, and share about it on your social media. You'll be surprised by whom God brings into your life to do the study with you.
- *Organize refreshments.* Hospitality is an important part of a group study. Oftentimes we provide snacks, coffee, and tea for the first session and then ask the other members to take turns providing the refreshments.
- *Plan the first meeting.* Take a moment to familiarize yourself with the format, making sure you can stream the videos and that you have all your materials ready. If you are doing this in an eight-week session, you will need to have everyone order their books ahead of time (autographed copies are available through thefriendshipprojectbook.com) and read the foreword, introduction, and chapter 1 before the first meeting. If you are distributing the books at the first gathering, you can read through the foreword and introduction together and use

the optional Introductory Session materials below. Or you can make it a little celebration and take the opportunity to get to know the other women over coffee and snacks. If you'd like to try some icebreakers, visit thefriendshipprojectbook.com for ideas. If providing the journal and other downloads for group members, be sure to make copies or e-mail out the links so the participants can print them.

Optional Introductory Session: Foreword and Introduction

Prayer to St. John the Apostle, patron saint of friendship:

> St. John, Glorious Apostle and much-loved disciple of Jesus, you were a faithful friend to Christ and stayed by his side through his Passion, Death, and Resurrection. Help me to be a good friend to others, and bring my friends close to the heart of Jesus.
>
> Please beg before the throne of God that I may be a friend of faith, hope, love, prudence, gratitude, loyalty, generosity, and prayerfulness and that friendships of virtue come into my life.
>
> St. John, please intercede before the throne of God that I may be blessed with faith-filled friendships that continue into eternity. Amen.

Watch the introductory video.

STUDY QUESTIONS

1. What did you learn from the reflection on friendship by Fr. Larry Richards in the foreword?
2. What is your thought on Michele's daughter's comment: "Why do we need friends anyway? We have our family, and we have TV"? What value do you see in friendship?
3. Do you agree with St. Augustine's quotation, "In this world two things are essential: life and friendship.

Both should be highly prized and we must not undervalue them. Life and friendship are nature's gifts"? Why or why not?

4. What are the three categories of friendship according to Aristotle? To what degree do you find these different types of friendships in your life?
5. Which type of friendship is most fulfilling to you? Which type of friendship is easiest for you to form? Describe a virtuous or spiritual friend and how that friend has made a difference in your life.

GOING DEEPER INTO SCRIPTURE

Prepare your hearts. Sit before God and pray: "Dear Lord, thank you for giving us your Word; help us to hear your voice and respond to your call. Amen."

Read the scripture slowly: "Whatever is true, whatever is honorable, whatever is just, whatever is pure, whatever is lovely, whatever is gracious, if there is any excellence, if there is anything worthy of praise, think about these things" (Phil 4:8).

1. Spend a moment in silence. What strikes you from this passage?
2. Re-read the scripture slowly. Then spend a moment in silence. What do you hear and see this time? How is God speaking to you?
3. Re-read the scripture for a third time. Then spend a moment in silence. How is God inviting you to change? Write down what you feel God is calling you to do.
4. Spend a moment giving thanks to God. Offer this simple prayer: "Dear Lord, thank you for this time spent with your Word. Thank you for speaking to our hearts. Please help us change the things in our lives we need to change and to follow your will. Amen."

Bonus Project: Take a few minutes to evaluate your friendships. Make a list of your friends in categories: utility, pleasure, virtuous and spiritual friends. As you read through *The Friendship Project*, jot down ideas you would like to try to deepen and develop these friendships. For a guide, download the "Friendship in Progress: Deepening and Developing Friendships" page at thefriendshipprojectbook.com.

Session 1: Chapter 1: Finding Faith

> Faith is the theological virtue by which we believe in God and believe all that he has said and revealed to us, and that Holy Church proposes for our belief, because he is truth itself. By faith "man freely commits his entire self to God." For this reason the believer seeks to know and do God's will.
>
> —*Catechism of the Catholic Church*, 1814

Open with the Holy Spirit Prayer:
> Come Holy Spirit, deepen my faith in you.
> Come Holy Spirit, show me how to be a friend of faith.
> Come Holy Spirit, bring me friends of faith.
> Sts. Gertrude and Matilda, pray for us.

Watch the Session 1 Video: Finding Faith.

STUDY QUESTIONS

1. Do you have anyone in your life with whom you feel comfortable sharing your faith? Why do you feel this way?
2. Has there been a time in your life when God has sent you a special friend when you needed it most? What happened?
3. How did you feel when you learned, either through this study or previously, that many saints were

friends on earth, helping each other along the journey? What impact did that knowledge have on you?
4. Have you ever heard of St. Matilda and St. Gertrude before? What strikes you about their story? What other saints do you know of who were friends on earth?
5. What are some obstacles to sharing your faith with others?

GOING DEEPER INTO SCRIPTURE

Prepare your hearts. Sit before God and pray: "Dear Lord, thank you for giving us your Word; help us to hear your voice and respond to your call. Amen."

Read the scripture slowly:

> Ask and it will be given to you; seek and you will find; knock and the door will be opened to you. For everyone who asks, receives; and the one who seeks, finds; and to the one who knocks, the door will be opened. Which one of you would hand his son a stone when he asks for a loaf of bread, or a snake when he asks for a fish? If you then, who are wicked, know how to give good gifts to your children, how much more will your heavenly Father give good things to those who ask him. (Mt 7:7–11)

1. Spend a moment in silence. What strikes you from this passage?
2. Re-read the scripture slowly. Then spend a moment in silence. What do you hear and see this time? How is God speaking to you?
3. Re-read the scripture for a third time. Then spend a moment in silence. How is God inviting you to change? Write down what you feel God is calling you to do.

4. Spend a moment giving thanks to God. Offer this
   simple prayer: "Dear Lord, thank you for this time
   spent with your Word. Thank you for speaking to
   our hearts. Please help us change the things in our
   lives we need to change and to follow your will.
   Amen."

End with the Prayer for Friends of Faith after inviting
your group to share their prayer intentions.

> Dear Lord,
> Please help me to grow in my Catholic faith so that
> I may seek your will in my life. Show me your face
> throughout my day, and teach me how to share
> my faith with others. I believe in you and want my
> friends to share the beautiful gift of knowing you. In
> scriptures you tell us, "Seek and you shall find, knock
> and the door shall open." Please bring me spiritual
> friends who will draw me closer to you and grant
> that I may do the same for them.
>   Sts. Matilda and Gertrude, pray for us.

Session 2: Chapter 2: Holding on to Hope

> Hope is the theological virtue by which we desire the
> kingdom of heaven and eternal life as our happiness,
> placing our trust in Christ's promises and relying not
> on our own strength, but on the help of the grace of
> the Holy Spirit.
>   —*Catechism of the Catholic Church*, 1817

Open with the Prayer to the Holy Spirit:

> Come Holy Spirit, deepen my hope in you.
> Come Holy Spirit, show me how to be a friend of
>   hope.
> Come Holy Spirit, bring me friends of hope.
> Sts. Perpetua and Felicity, pray for us.

Watch the Session 2 Video: Holding on to Hope.

STUDY QUESTIONS

1. What did you think of Stacey's story of hope?
2. Stacey shared that Christ revealed himself to her as a friend during her darkest hour. Do you see Christ as your friend, especially when you are going through times of trial and loneliness?
3. Do you see value in suffering? Why do you feel that way? Have you ever experienced suffering where it has transformed you and made you a better person?
4. Had you ever heard of Sts. Perpetua and Felicity? What do you think of their story? Have you ever had a friend help you in a heroic way? Describe your experience.
5. Do you think of hope as a virtue, or do you see it more as the secular view of optimism? In what ways?
6. Have you ever come up against an obstacle to hope such as despair? What did you do? Did a friend of hope help you overcome this difficulty? Describe this experience.

GOING DEEPER INTO SCRIPTURE

Prepare your hearts. Sit before God and pray: "Dear Lord, thank you for giving us your Word; help us to hear your voice and respond to your call. Amen."

Read the scripture slowly: "We who have taken refuge might be strongly encouraged to hold fast to the hope that lies before us. This we have as an anchor of the soul, sure and firm, which reaches into the interior behind the veil" (Heb 6:18–19).

1. Spend a moment in silence. What strikes you from this passage?
2. Re-read the scripture slowly. Then spend a moment in silence. What do you hear and see this time? How is God speaking to you?

3. Re-read the scripture for a third time. Then spend a moment in silence. How is God inviting you to change? Write down what you feel God is calling you to do.

4. Spend a moment giving thanks to God. Offer this simple prayer: "Dear Lord, thank you for this time spent with your Word. Thank you for speaking to our hearts. Please help us change the things in our lives we need to change and to follow your will. Amen."

End with the Prayer for Friends of Hope after inviting your group to share their prayer intentions.

> Dear Lord,
> Help me to grow in the virtue of hope. Help me to desire the kingdom of heaven and eternal life as my happiness and to place my trust in Christ's promises, not relying on my own strength but on the grace of the Holy Spirit. Help me to profess that Jesus is Lord and bring the virtue of hope to others, especially the hopeless. Lord, please bring me hope-filled friends who will draw me closer to you, and grant that I may do the same for them.
> Sts. Perpetua and Felicity, pray for us.

Session 3: Chapter 3: Cultivating Charity

> Charity is the theological virtue by which we love God above all things for his own sake, and our neighbor as ourselves for the love of God.
> —*Catechism of the Catholic Church*, 1822

Open with the Prayer to the Holy Spirit:

> Come Holy Spirit, deepen my love for You.
> Come Holy Spirit, show me how to be a friend of love.

Come Holy Spirit, bring me friends of love.
St. Thérèse of Lisieux and Servant of God Léonie
Martin, pray for us.

Watch the Session 3 Video: Cultivating Charity.

STUDY QUESTIONS

1. Have you ever been the recipient or giver of a gift of love to a friend? How did it make you feel? Did it strengthen your faith and deepen the bond of your friendship? If so, in what ways?

2. What do you think of the quote by St. Aelred of Rievaulx: "The source and origin of friendship is love. Although love can exist without friendship, friendship cannot exist without love"? Do you think this is true? Why do you feel that way?

3. What is the link between charity and prayer? Reflect on this statement from the book: "Charity requires practice fueled by prayer to obtain the graces I need to live out this virtue." How do you see this lived out practically?

4. In this chapter, we see the love and friendship of two sisters, St. Thérèse of Lisieux and Servant of God Léonie Martin. Did you know about their friendship? What do you think of their story? Do you see the possibility of developing and deepening friendships in your family? Or do you find the quote from St. Teresa of Calcutta true: "It is easy to love people far away. It is not always easy to love those close to us"?

5. Have you ever declined God's promptings to perform a kind deed or offer a word or prayer for a friend out of love? What did you do?

GOING DEEPER INTO SCRIPTURE

Prepare your hearts. Sit before God and pray: "Dear Lord, thank you for giving us your Word; help us to hear your voice and respond to your call. Amen."

Read the scripture slowly: "Love is patient, love is kind. It is not jealous, it is not pompous, it is not inflated, it is not rude, it does not seek its own interests, it is not quick tempered, it does not brood over injury, it does not rejoice over wrongdoing but rejoices with the truth. It bears all things, believes all things, hopes all things, endures all things. Love never fails" (1 Cor 13:4–8).

1. Spend a moment in silence. What strikes you from this passage?
2. Re-read the scripture slowly. Then spend a moment in silence. What do you hear and see this time? How is God speaking to you?
3. Re-read the scripture for a third time. Then spend a moment in silence. How is God inviting you to change? Write down what you feel God is calling you to do.
4. Spend a moment giving thanks to God. Offer this simple prayer: "Dear Lord, thank you for this time spent with your Word. Thank you for speaking to our hearts. Please help us change the things in our lives we need to change and to follow your will. Amen."

End with the Prayer for Friends of Charity after inviting your group to share their prayer intentions.

Dear Lord,
Help me to grow in the virtue of charity. Help me to love you above all things for your own sake, and my neighbor as myself for the love of you. Protect me from the vices that destroy love in friendship. Help me to be patient and kind and to rejoice in true

friendship. Please protect me from gossip, slander, jealousy, rudeness, and any other vice that destroys friendship. Lord, please bring me friends filled with love who will draw me closer to you and grant that I may do the same for them.

St. Thérèse of Lisieux and Servant of God Léonie Martin, pray for us.

Session 4: Chapter 4: Practicing Prudence

Prudence is the virtue that disposes practical reason to discern our true good in every circumstance and to choose the right means of achieving it

—*Catechism of the Catholic Church*, 1806

Open with the Prayer to the Holy Spirit:

Come Holy Spirit, deepen the virtue of prudence in my life.

Come Holy Spirit, show me how to be a prudent friend.

Come Holy Spirit, bring me friends who exemplify the virtue of prudence.

St. Hildegard of Bingen, Doctor of the Church, and Bl. Jutta, pray for us.

Watch the Session 4 Video: Practicing Prudence.

STUDY QUESTIONS

1. Have you ever been in a difficult situation similar to Emily's in which your possible lack of prudence led to isolation and you needed to reset your life? Did you ever consider how the virtue of prudence can be a beacon of light helping you balance your relationships with your other obligations? What are your thoughts on this?

2. Were you familiar with the story of St. Hildegard of Bingen and Bl. Jutta? What do you think about their friendship? Do you have a friendship or relationship

with someone at your parish (priest, religious sister, deacon, or lay religious) or in your life whom you can call on to seek counsel and call friend?

3. Were you familiar with St. Thomas Aquinas's formula for making a prudent decision (self-evaluation, seeking counsel, and decisiveness)? Could this formula be helpful to you in making choices in your life? In what ways?

4. What about the pitfalls St. Thomas Aquinas mentions: impulse, passion, and stubbornness? How could these affect your friendships, especially in the digital age?

5. As the spiritual director of St. Hildegard, Bl. Jutta helped her friend discover God's will in her life and maximize her time and talents for the Lord while always investing in a deep and rich prayer life. Do you have friendships that allow you to realize your potential? How can they help you grow into the person God wants you to be? If you don't have such friendships yet, what might you do to develop one?

GOING DEEPER INTO SCRIPTURE

Prepare your hearts. Sit before God and pray: "Dear Lord, thank you for giving us your Word; help us to hear your voice and respond to your call. Amen."

Read the scripture slowly: "Come to me, all you who labor and are burdened, and I will give you rest. Take my yoke upon you and learn from me, for I am meek and humble of heart; and you will find rest for yourselves. For my yoke is easy, and my burden light" (Mt 11: 28–30).

1. Spend a moment in silence. What strikes you from this passage?

2. Re-read the scripture slowly. Then spend a moment in silence. What do you hear and see this time? How is God speaking to you?

3. Re-read the scripture for a third time. Then spend a moment in silence. How is God inviting you to change? Write down what you feel God is calling you to do.

4. Spend a moment giving thanks to God. Offer this simple prayer: "Dear Lord, thank you for this time spent with your Word. Thank you for speaking to our hearts. Please help us change the things in our lives we need to change and to follow your will. Amen."

End with the Prayer for Friends of Prudence after inviting your group to share their prayer intentions.

> Dear Lord,
> Help me to grow in the virtue of prudence. Help me to discern true good in every circumstance and to choose the right means of achieving it. Help me to maximize my time and talents for you, Lord, and avoid acting out of impulse, passion, or stubbornness. Please bring me friends filled with the virtue of prudence who will draw me closer to you and grant that I may do the same for them.
> St. Hildegard of Bingen, Doctor of the Church, and Bl. Jutta, pray for us.

Session 5: Chapter 5: Growing in Gratitude

> [Gratitude is a] thankful disposition of mind and heart.
> —"Gratitude," *Education in Virtue*

Open with the Prayer to the Holy Spirit:

> Come Holy Spirit, deepen the virtue of gratitude in my life.

Come Holy Spirit, show me how to be a grateful
friend.
Come Holy Spirit, bring me friends who are grateful.
St. Teresa of Avila, Doctor of the Church, and Bl.
Anne of St. Bartholomew, pray for us.

Watch the Session 5 Video: Growing in Gratitude.

STUDY QUESTIONS

1. Have you ever gone through a difficult situation in
    which God opened your eyes to the virtue of grat-
    itude, of being thankful for all that you have been
    given? Does your attitude affect your ability to be
    grateful? Explain.
2. What do you think of the quotation from Alice Von
    Hildebrand, "Gratitude is the blessed oil on which
    friendship and marriage thrive"? Have you experi-
    enced this?
3. What did you think of the friendship of St. Teresa of
    Avila and Bl. Anne of St. Bartholomew? Theirs was
    one of selfless service. We may be called to serve in
    our friendships: How do we grow in gratitude in
    the midst of helping another friend? What are some
    healthy boundaries for situations like these? What
    might a friend do to prevent resentment?
4. One of the biggest obstacles to gratitude is compar-
    ison. What do you think about the quote from St.
    Teresa of Avila: "Never compare one person with
    another: comparisons are odious"? Do you find that
    comparison is a roadblock in your friendships? If so,
    what can you do? If not, why do you think it's not
    an issue?
5. How might materialism keep you from being grate-
    ful? Do you think if you had less you would be more
    grateful? If you have the opportunity, watch the
    video mentioned in the chapter about the Haitians

dancing and praising God after the earthquake. Find the video at https://www.youtube.com/ watch?v=5zIstG23dVQ. Do you think you could have this attitude of gratitude? What evidence from your past—or insight you've gained for your future—tells you this?

GOING DEEPER INTO SCRIPTURE

Prepare your hearts. Sit before God and pray: "Dear Lord, thank you for giving us your Word; help us to hear your voice and respond to your call. Amen."

Read the scripture slowly: "Have no anxiety at all . . . let the peace of Christ control your hearts, the peace into which you were also called in one body. And be thankful. Let the word of Christ dwell in you richly, as in all wisdom you teach and admonish one another, singing psalms, hymns, and spiritual songs with gratitude in your hearts to God. And whatever you do, in word or in deed, do everything in the name of the Lord Jesus, giving thanks to God the Father through him" (Col 3:15–17).

1. Spend a moment in silence. What strikes you from this passage?
2. Re-read the scripture slowly. Then spend a moment in silence. What do you hear and see this time? How is God speaking to you?
3. Re-read the scripture for a third time. Then spend a moment in silence. How is God inviting you to change? Write down what you feel God is calling you to do.
4. Spend a moment giving thanks to God. Offer this simple prayer: "Dear Lord, thank you for this time spent with your Word. Thank you for speaking to our hearts. Please help us change the things in our

lives we need to change and to follow your will. Amen."

End with the Prayer for Friends of Gratitude after inviting your group to share their prayer intentions.

Dear Lord,
Help me to grow in the virtue of gratitude. Please help me develop a thankful disposition of mind and heart. Help me to praise you always, even when things are difficult. Help me to be grateful for my friends and to do small acts of service for them, showing my appreciation through my actions. Shield my friendships from comparison, envy, and unforgiveness. Lord, please bring me friends filled with gratitude who will draw me closer to you and grant that I may do the same for them.

St. Teresa of Avila, Doctor of the Church, and Bl. Anne of St. Bartholomew, pray for us.

Session 6: Chapter 6: Living Loyalty

[Loyalty is] accepting the bonds implicit in relationships and defending the virtues upheld by Church, family, and country.
—"Loyalty," *Education in Virtue*

Open with the Prayer to the Holy Spirit:

Come Holy Spirit, deepen the virtue of loyalty in my life.
Come Holy Spirit, show me how to be a loyal friend.
Come Holy Spirit, bring me loyal friends.
Ruth and Naomi, pray for us.

Watch the Session 6 Video: Living Loyalty.

STUDY QUESTIONS

1. Can you think of an encounter of loyalty in your friendships? How is loyalty in friendship different

than showing your approval or acceptance of another's actions?

2. Loyalty is putting our friends ahead of ourselves and may mean making a sacrifice. In life, we need to learn how to remain loyal to the people, places, and duties to which God has asked us to be faithful. How has God asked you to remain loyal even in difficult situations? How can friendships teach us about loyalty? What is the role of boundaries in loyal friendships?

3. We see in scripture that even Christ's friends, such as St. Peter, were disloyal to him. What do you think of the quote, "Peter got his loyalties confused when he took his eyes off Christ"? How can we be become weak and vulnerable when we take our eyes off Jesus?

4. Were you familiar with the biblical story of Ruth and Naomi? This story of loyalty and friendship from the book of Ruth is a great reminder of the impact we can have on others through being a faithful and spiritual friend. Do you have someone in your life like Naomi? Or are you Naomi to someone else?

5. How can you help yourself or others break the cycle of being a frenemy? In what ways can or do you avoid or overcome the temptation to gossip, slander, or spread rumors about your friends?

GOING DEEPER INTO SCRIPTURE

Prepare your hearts. Sit before God and pray: "Dear Lord, thank you for giving us your Word; help us to hear your voice and respond to your call. Amen."

Read the scripture slowly:

> Faithful friends are a sturdy shelter;
>   whoever finds one finds a treasure.
> Faithful friends are beyond price,

no amount can balance their worth.
Faithful friends are life-saving medicine;
those who fear God will find them. (Sir 6:14–16)

1. Spend a moment in silence. What strikes you from this passage?
2. Re-read the scripture slowly. Then spend a moment in silence. What do you hear and see this time? How is God speaking to you?
3. Re-read the scripture for a third time. Then spend a moment in silence. How is God inviting you to change? Write down what you feel God is calling you to do.
4. Spend a moment giving thanks to God. Offer this simple prayer: "Dear Lord, thank you for this time spent with your Word. Thank you for speaking to our hearts. Please help us change the things in our lives we need to change and to follow your will. Amen."

End with the Prayer for Friends of Loyalty after inviting your group to share their prayer intentions.

Dear Lord,
Help me to grow in the virtue of loyalty. Please help me develop loyalty in all my relationships and defend the virtues upheld by the Church, my family, and my country. Help me to remain faithful, even when things are difficult. Help me to be loyal to my spouse, family, dear friends, and employers and to exhibit stability. Shield my friendships from disloyalty, betrayal, and judgments. Lord, please bring me loyal friends who will draw me closer to you and grant that I may do the same for them.
Ruth and Naomi, pray for us.

Session 7: Chapter 7: Giving Generosity

[Generosity is] giving of oneself in a willing and cheerful manner for the good of others.

—"Generosity," *Education in Virtue*

Open with the Prayer to the Holy Spirit:

Come Holy Spirit, deepen the virtue of generosity in me.

Come Holy Spirit, show me how to be a generous friend.

Come Holy Spirit, bring me friends who serve you generously.

Sts. Catherine of Siena and Catherine of Sweden, pray for us.

Watch the Session 7 Video: Giving Generosity.

STUDY QUESTIONS

1. Have you ever given a little yes to God that blossomed into a friendship? How did it happen?
2. What do you think about the scripture that tells us that "it is more blessed to give than to receive" (Acts 20:35)? Can you think of a time in which you felt blessed to give of yourself? How did that affect you? Has it affected your attitude of generosity?
3. We shared the quote from St. John Paul II: "In the designs of Providence, there are no mere coincidences." In light of this quote, have you ever had an experience like Michele had at the Shrine of Christ's Passion?
4. Were you familiar with the story of St. Catherine of Siena and St. Catherine of Sweden? Has a friend ever inspired you or helped you do something really big for God like we heard in the story of two St. Catherines?

5. In a very self-centered culture, it can be easy to fall
    victim to selfishness. Do you have any friends that
    help you become more generous and less likely to
    think about yourself?
6. Pope Benedict XVI reminds us of the importance
    of hospitality, "which has almost disappeared." Do
    you agree with this quote? Do you think this virtue
    can enhance your friendships?

GOING DEEPER INTO SCRIPTURE

Prepare your hearts. Sit before God and pray: "Dear
Lord, thank you for giving us your Word; help us to
hear your voice and respond to your call. Amen."

    Read the scripture slowly: "I no longer call you
slaves, because a slave does not know what his master
is doing. I have called you friends" (Jn 15:15).

1. Spend a moment in silence. What strikes you from
    this passage?
2. Re-read the scripture slowly. Then spend a moment
    in silence. What do you hear and see this time? How
    is God speaking to you?
3. Re-read the scripture for a third time. Then spend
    a moment in silence. How is God inviting you to
    change? Write down what you feel God is calling
    you to do.
4. Spend a moment giving thanks to God. Offer this
    simple prayer: "Dear Lord, thank you for this time
    spent with your Word. Thank you for speaking to
    our hearts. Please help us change the things in our
    lives we need to change and to follow your will.
    Amen."

End with the Prayer for Friends of Generosity after
inviting your group to share their prayer intentions.

Dear Lord,

Help me to grow in the virtue of generosity. Please help me give of myself in a willing and cheerful manner for the good of others. Help me to be a generous friend by giving from what you have given me. Help me to be generous always, even when my generosity is misunderstood. Shield my friendships from selfishness, stinginess, and ingratitude. Lord, please bring me friends filled with generosity who will draw me closer to you and grant that I may do the same for them.

St. Catherine of Siena, Doctor of the Church, and St. Catherine of Sweden, pray for us.

Session 8: Chapter 8: Pondering Prayerfulness

[Prayer is having a] personal relationship with the living and true God. . . . "Prayer is the raising of one's mind and heart to God or the requesting of good things from God."

—*Catechism of the Catholic Church*, 2558–2559

Open with the Prayer to the Holy Spirit:

Come Holy Spirit, deepen the virtue of prayerfulness in me.

Come Holy Spirit, show me how to be a prayerful friend.

Come Holy Spirit, bring me friends who pray.

Holy Mary, Mother of God, and St. Elizabeth, pray for us.

Watch the Session 8 Video: Pondering Prayerfulness.

STUDY QUESTIONS

1. What do you think of the advice from Emily's brother, Fr. Jonathan, "You can't afford not to pray"?

Do you think prayer is a necessity for living a Christian life? Why do you feel that way?

2. Have you prayed with a friend? If so, what was that experience like for you?

3. Ephrem of Syria tells us, "Virtues are formed by prayer. Prayer preserves self-control. Prayer suppresses anger. Prayer prevents emotions of pride and envy. Prayer draws into the soul the Holy Spirit, and raises man and woman to Heaven." Do you see a link between prayer and growing in virtue? What has been your experience of this in your life?

4. Were you familiar with the story of the friendship of the Blessed Mother and St. Elizabeth? What strikes you about that story? When we choose to allow other women into our lives and develop spiritual friendships, we are blessed beyond our imagination. How has spiritual friendship blessed you in your life? Can you see a value in these types of friendships?

5. Have you ever leaned on anyone for their prayers and the connection deepened into a friendship? St. Gregory shares with us that "we are linked by the power of prayer, we, as it were, hold each other's hand as we walk side by side along a slippery path; and thus by the bounteous disposition of charity, it comes about that the harder each one leans on the other, the more firmly we are riveted together in brotherly love."

GOING DEEPER INTO SCRIPTURE

Prepare your hearts. Sit before God and pray: "Dear Lord, thank you for giving us your Word; help us to hear your voice and respond to your call. Amen."

Read the scripture slowly: "And Mary said:

'My soul proclaims the greatness of the Lord;
my spirit rejoices in God my savior.
For he has looked upon his handmaid's lowliness;
behold, from now on will all ages call me blessed.'"
(Lk 1: 46–48)

1. Spend a moment in silence. What strikes you from this passage?
2. Re-read the scripture slowly. Then spend a moment in silence. What do you hear and see this time? How is God speaking to you?
3. Re-read the scripture for a third time. Then spend a moment in silence. How is God inviting you to change? Write down what you feel God is calling you to do.
4. Spend a moment giving thanks to God. Offer this simple prayer: "Dear Lord, thank you for this time spent with your Word. Thank you for speaking to our hearts. Please help us change the things in our lives we need to change and to follow your will. Amen."

End with the Prayer for Friends of Prayerfulness after inviting your group to share their prayer intentions.

Dear Lord,
Help me to grow in the virtue of prayerfulness. Please help me to develop and deepen my personal relationship with you. Help me to be prayerful even when I don't feel like it. Help me to pray for my friends, especially those who need my prayers the most. Bless my friends, and help me to reach out to others in a prayerful spirit. Lord, please bring me friends filled with the virtue of prayerfulness and who will draw me closer to you and grant that I may do the same for them.
Holy Mary, Mother of God, and St. Elizabeth, pray for us.

Notes

Introduction

1. Augustine, "Augustine's Words on Friendship," *Augnet*, accessed October 27, 2016, http://augnet.org/default.asp?ipageid=1657.

2. Jeanna Bryner, "Close Friends Less Common Today, Study Finds," *LiveScience*, November 4, 2011, http://www.livescience.com/16879-close-friends-decrease-today.html.

3. Jane Collingwood, "The Importance of Friendship," *Psych Central*, May 17, 2016, https://psychcentral.com/lib/the-importance-of-friendship.

4. Aristotle, *Nicomachean Ethics*, trans. W. D. Ross, 8.3, accessed February 8, 2017, http://classics.mit.edu/Aristotle/nicomachaen.8.viii.html.

5. Wendy M. Wright, *Francis de Sales: Introduction to the Devout Life and Treatise on the Love* (Stella Niagra, NY: DeSales Resource Center, 2005), 98.

6. Aelred of Rievaulx, *Aelred of Rievaulx: Spiritual Friendship*, trans. Lawrence C. Braceland, ed. Marsha L. Dutton (Collegeville, MN: Cistercian Publications, 2010), 57.

7. Andre Marie, M.I.C.M., "Friends Forever: St. Augustine, Friendship, and Catholic Evangelism," *Catholicism.org*, accessed October 27, 2016, http://catholicism.org/downloads/St_Augustine_Friendship.pdf.

8. Francisco Fernández-Carvajal, *In Conversation with God*, vol. 2 (New York: Scepter Publishers, 1989), 498.

1. Finding Faith

1. Franciscan University of Steubenville, "Faith Households: 40 Years of Christ-Centered Friendship," accessed October 28, 2016, http://www.franciscan.edu/Households.

2. Tadeusz Dajczer, *The Gift of Faith* (Fort Collins, CO: In the Arms of Mary Foundation, 2011), 1.

3. John A. Hardon, S.J., "The Virtue of Faith," *The Real Presence*, July 13, 1998, accessed October 29, 2016, http://www.therealpresence.org/archives/Holy_Spirit/Holy_Spirit_010.htm.

4. Teresa of Avila, *The Collected Works of St. Teresa of Avila*, trans. Kieran Kavanaugh, O.C.D., and Otilio Rodriguez, O.C.D., vol. 1 (Washington, DC: ICS Publications, 1976), 64–65.

5. Carol Kelly-Gangi, ed., *The Essential Wisdom of the Saints* (New York: Fall River Press, 2008), 98.

6. Benedict XVI, General Audience: St. Matilda of Hackeborn, September 29, 2010, accessed October 29, 2016, https://w2.vatican.va/content/benedict-xvi/en/audiences/2010/documents/hf_ben-xvi_aud_20100929.html.

7. Gertrude the Great, as quoted in Benedict XVI, General Audience: St. Gertrude the Great, October 6, 2010, accessed January 20, 2017, w2.vatican.va/content/benedict-xvi/en/audiences/2010/documents/hf_ben-xvi_aud_20101006.html.

8. Benedict XVI, General Audience: St. Matilda of Hackeborn, https://w2.vatican.va/content/benedict-xvi/en/audiences/2010/documents/hf_ben-xvi_aud_20100929.html.

9. Ibid.

10. Francis, General Audience, April 10, 2013, http://w2.vatican.va/content/francesco/en/audiences/2013/documents/papa-francesco_20130410_udienza-generale.html.

2. Holding on to Hope

1. "Eucharistic Prayer I (Roman Canon)," *The Roman Missal* (Collegeville, MN: Liturgical Press, 2011), 642.

2. "Sts. Perpetua and Felicity," *Catholic Online*, accessed October 15, 2016, http://www.catholic.org/saints/saint.php?saint_id=48.

3. "Eucharistic Prayer I (Roman Canon)," 642.

4. Ibid.

5. "Sts. Perpetua and Felicity," *Catholic Online*, http://www.catholic.org/saints/saint.php?saint_id=48.

6. "The Passion of the Holy Martyrs Perpetua and Felicity," trans. by R. E. Wallis, in *Ante-Nicene Fathers*, ed. by Alexander Roberts, James Donaldson, and A. Cleveland Coxe, vol. 3 (Buffalo, NY: Christian Literature Publishing Co., 1885). Revised and edited for *New Advent* by Kevin Knight, http://www.newadvent.org/fathers/0324.htm.

7. "Sts. Perpetua and Felicity," *Catholic Online*, http://www.catholic.org/saints/saint.php?saint_id=48.

8. Francis, General Audience, April 10, 2013, http://w2.vatican.va/content/francesco/en/audiences/2013/documents/papa-francesco_20130410_udienza-generale.html.

9. Francis, Papal Homily at Holy Mass in the Basilica of the Shrine of Our Lady of the Conception of Aparecida, July 24, 2013, accessed January 20, 2017, http://w2.vatican.va/content/francesco/en/homilies/2013/documents/papa-francesco_20130724_gmg-omelia-aparecida.html.

3. Cultivating Charity

1. Catherine of Siena, *The Dialogue of the Seraphic Virgin: Catherine of Siena*, trans. Algar Thorold (Potosi, WI: St. Athanasius Press, 2014), 15–16.

2. Jamil Zaki, "What, Me Care? Young Are Less Empathetic," *Scientific American*, December 23, 2010, accessed October 29, 2016, http://www.scientificamerican.com/article/what-me-care/?page=1.

3. Francis W. Johnston, *The Voice of the Saints: Counsels from the Saints to Bring Comfort and Guidance in Daily Living* (Rockford, IL: TAN Books and Publishers, 1986), 27.

4. Aelred of Rievaulx, *Aelred of Rievaulx: Spiritual Friendship*, 98.

5. Susan Conroy, *Praying with Mother Teresa: Prayers, Insights, and Wisdom of Saint Teresa of Calcutta* (Stockbridge, MA: Marian Press, 2016), 36.

6. Teresa of Avila, *The Collected Works of St. Teresa of Avila*, trans. Kieran Kavanaugh, O.C.D., and Otilio Rodriguez, O.C.D., vol. 2 (Washington, DC: ICS Publications, 1976), 353.

7. "Her Life at Lisieux Carmel," Society of the Little Flower, accessed October 29, 2016, http://www.littleflower.org/therese/life-story/her-life-at-lisieux-carmel.

8. Thérèse of Lisieux, *Story of a Soul: The Autobiography of St. Thérèse of Lisieux*, trans. John Clarke, 2nd ed. (Washington, DC: ICS Publications, 1996), 156.

9. Ibid., 207.

10. Maureen O'Riordan, "Léonie Martin, Disciple and Sister of St. Thérèse of Lisieux," accessed October 29, 2016, http://leoniemartin.org/visitation-booklet.

11. Ibid.

12. Thérèse of Lisieux, *Story of a Soul*, 23.

13. O'Riordan, "Léonie Martin, Disciple and Sister of St. Thérèse of Lisieux," http://leoniemartin.org/visitation-booklet.

14. Léonie Martin, "From Sr. Francoise—Thérèse (Léonie) to Her Three Sisters—February 2, 1899," *Archives du Carmel de Lisieux*, accessed October 29, 2016, http://www.archives-carmel-lisieux.fr/english/carmel/index.php/soeur-francoise-therese-leonie/19139-from-sr-francoise-therese-leonie-to-her-three-sisters-february-2-1899.

15. O'Riordan, "Léonie Martin, Disciple and Sister of St. Thérèse of Lisieux," http://leoniemartin.org/visitation-booklet.

16. Thérèse of Lisieux, *Story of a Soul*, 127.

17. Francis, Angelus Address, February 16, 2014, accessed October 29, 2016, https://w2.vatican.va/content/francesco/en/angelus/2014/documents/papa-francesco_angelus_20140216.html.

18. Ibid.

19. Paul Anthony Melanson, "Dr. Alice von Hildebrand on Hypersensitivity," *La Salette Journey* (blog), January 30, 2007, accessed October 29, 2016, http://lasalettejourney.blogspot.com/2007/01/dr-alice-von-hildebrand-on.html.

20. Francis, General Audience, October 22, 2014, https://w2.vatican.va/content/francesco/en/audiences/2014/documents/papa-francesco_20141022_udienza-generale.html.

21. Ibid.

22. Ambrose, "On the Duties of the Clergy (Book III)," *New Advent*, ch. 3, sec. 131, accessed October 29, 2016, http://www.newadvent.org/fathers/34013.htm.

4. Practicing Prudence

1. "Prudence," *Catholic News Agency*, accessed August 5, 2016, http://www.catholicnewsagency.com/resources/virtue/cardinal-virtues/prudence.

2. "Glossary" in *Catechism of the Catholic Church*, 2nd ed. (Vatican City: Libreria Editrice Vaticana, 2000), s.v. "virtue."

3. St. Joseph Catholic Church, "Lesson 27—The Cardinal Virtue of Prudence," accessed September 2, 2016, http://www.sjohio.org/assets/templates/mycustom/ethereal/files/lesson/holyspirit/Lesson27ATheCardinal-Virtueof%20Prudence.pdf.

4. Augustine, "On the Customs of the Catholic Church," as quoted in Fernández-Carvajal, *In Conversation with God*, 106.

5. Thomas Aquinas, *Summa Theologiae*, 2-2, question 49, article 3, accessed September 5, 2016, http://www.newadvent.org/summa/3047.htm.

6. Josemaría Escrivá, *Friends of God: Homilies* (London: Scepter Publishing, 1981), 86.

7. Francisco Fernández-Carvajal, *In Conversation with God*, vol. 4 (London: Scepter Publishing, 1997), 102.

8. Anne King-Lenzmier, *Hildegard of Bingen: An Integrated Vision* (Collegeville, MN: Liturgical Press, 2001), 198.

9. Edward P. Sri, "The Art of Living: The First Step of Prudence," *Lay Witness* (May/June 2009), accessed August 15, 2016, http://www.catholiceducation.org/en/education/virtue-education/the-art-of-living-the-first-step-of-prudence.html.

10. William Saunders, "Prudence: Mother of All Virtues," *Arlington Catholic Herald*, accessed August 21, 2016, http://www.catholiceducation.org/en/culture/catholic-contributions/prudence-mother-of-all-virtues.html.

11. Fernández-Carvajal, *In Conversation with God*, vol. 4, 109.

12. Russell Shaw, "Prudence: The Forgotten Christian Virtue," accessed August 29, 2016, www.osv.com/MyFaith/ModelsoftheFaith/Article/TabId/684/Art-MID/13728/ArticleID/4344/Prudence-the-forgotten-Christian-virtue.aspxage.

13. Benedict XVI, "Apostolic Letter Proclaiming Saint Hildegard of Bingen, Professed Nun of the Order of Saint Benedict, a Doctor of the Universal Church," accessed August 28, 2016, w2.vatican.va/content/benedict-xvi/en/apost_letters/documents/hf_ben-xvi_apl_20121007_ildegarda-bingen.html.

14. Susan Abernethy, "Hildegard of Bingen," *The Freelance History Writer* (blog), August 16, 2013, accessed August 28, 2016, https://thefreelancehistorywriter.com/tag/jutta-of-sponheim.

15. Heinrich Schipperges, *Hildegard of Bingen: Healing and the Nature of the Cosmos* (Princeton, NJ: Markus Wiener Publishers, 1997), 10.

16. Gerelyn Hollingsworth, "On This Day: Blessed Jutta, OSB," *National Catholic Reporter*, December 22, 2010, https://www.ncronline.org/blogs/ncr-today/day-blessed-jutta-osb.

17. Benedict XVI, "Apostolic Letter Proclaiming Hildegard of Bingen, Professed Nun of the Order of Saint Benedict, a Doctor of the Universal Church," w2.vatican.va/content/benedict-xvi/en/apost_letters/documents/hf_ben-xvi_apl_20121007_ildegarda-bingen.html.

18. Ibid.

19. Janice Shaw Crouse, "The Loneliness of American Society," *The American Spectator*, ed. R. Emmett Tyrrell Jr., May 18, 2014, https://spectator.org/59230_loneliness-american-society.

20. Jeff Arrowood, "Too Busy? 4 Ways the Virtue of Prudence Can Help," accessed January 20, 2017, http://www.fromtheabbey.com/keys-entryway-virtue-prudence/too-busy-prudence-conquers-busyness-overload.

21. Sri, "The Art of Living," *Lay Witness*, http://www.catholiceducation.org/en/education/virtue-education/the-art-of-living-the-first-step-of-prudence.html.

5. Growing in Gratitude

1. Anne of St. Bartholomew, *Autobiography of the Blessed Mother Anne of Saint Bartholomew, Inseparable Companion of Saint Teresa and Foundress of the Carmels of Pontoise, Tours, and Antwerp* (St. Louis, MO: H. S. Collins Printing, 1916), 45.

2. Teresa of Avila, *The Collected Works of St. Teresa of Avila*, vol. 2, 313.

3. Frederick F. Campbell, "Bishop Campbell Reflections: Scripture Verses That Strike You More Deeply; 1st Sunday in Lent," *St. Gabriel Catholic Radio*, February 16, 2016, accessed January 20, 2017, http://stgabrielradio.com/021616-weekly-reflection.

4. Elise Harris, "When Was the Last Time You Said 'Thank You' and 'I'm Sorry'? Pope Asks," *Catholic News Agency*, May 13, 2013, accessed October 29, 2016, http://www.catholicnewsagency.com/news/when-was-the-last-time-you-said-thank-you-and-im-sorry-pope-asks-12071.

5. Fernández-Carvajal, *In Conversation with God*, vol. 2, 443.

6. Alice von Hildebrand, "The Canons of Friendship," Catholic Culture, May 2006, accessed October 29, 2016, https://www.catholicculture.org/culture/library/view.cfm?recnum=7125.

7. Teresa of Avila, *The Complete Works of St. Teresa of Avila*, trans. E. Allison Peers, vol. 3 (London: Burns and Oates, 2002), 258.

8. Teresa of Avila, *The Collected Works of St. Teresa of Avila*, vol. 2, 47.

9. Teresa of Avila, *The Complete Works of St. Teresa of Avila*, vol. 1, 36–37.

10. Ibid., 37.

11. Teresa of Avila, *The Collected Works of St. Teresa of Avila*, vol. 1, 5.

12. Anne of St. Bartholomew, *Autobiography of the Blessed Mother Anne of Saint Bartholomew*, 41.

13. Teresa of Avila, *The Life of St. Teresa of Jesus, of the Order of Our Lady of Carmel, Written by Herself*, trans. David Lewis, ed. Benedict Zimmerman, O.C.D., 3rd ed. (Westminster, MD: Newman Book Shop, 1947), Kindle edition.

14. Anne of St. Bartholomew, *Autobiography of the Blessed Mother Anne of Saint Bartholomew*, 38.

15. Robert F. McNamara, "Bl. Anne of Saint Bartholomew," St. Kateri Parish, accessed October 29, 2016, http://www.kateriirondequoit.org/resources/saints-alive/abercius-augustine-of-canterbury/bl-anne-of-saint-bartholomew.

16. Teresa of Avila, *The Complete Works of St. Teresa of Avila*, vol. 3, 256.

17. Emer McCarthy, "Pope at Audience: The Church, the Body of Christ," *Vatican Radio*, October 22, 2014, accessed January 20, 2017, http://en.radiovaticana.va/news/2014/10/22/pope_at_audience_the_church,_the_body_of_christ_/1109146.

18. "Haitians Singing Praise in Port-au-Prince Haiti after Earthquake," February 2, 2010, accessed October 29, 2016, https://www.youtube.com/watch?v=5zIstG23dVQ.

19. Mary DeTurris Poust, "Be Intentional, Be Prayerful, Be Humble: Three Steps to a More Grateful Life," *OSV Newsweekly*, November 17, 2014, accessed October 29, 2016, https://www.osv.com/OSVNewsweekly/InFocus/Article/TabId/721/ArtMID/13629/ArticleID/16399/Gratitude.aspx.

20. Baylor University, "Gratitude, Not 'Gimme,' Makes for More Satisfaction, Study Finds," *ScienceDaily*, March 31, 2014, accessed October 29, 2016, www.sciencedaily.com/releases/2014/03/140331180613.htm.

21. Francis, Holy Mass on the Occasion of the Marian Day on the Occasion of the Year of Faith of Holy Father Francis, October 13, 2013, accessed October 29, 2016, http://w2.vatican.va/content/francesco/en/homilies/2013/documents/papa-francesco_20131013_omelia-giornata-mariana.html.

22. Teresa of Avila, *The Collected Works of St. Teresa of Avila*, vol. 1, 173.

6. Living Loyalty

1. "Loyalty," *Virtue First Foundation*, accessed October 15, 2016, http://virtuefirst.org/virtues/loyalty.

2. "Virtue 101: Loyalty," *Regnum Christi*, accessed September 27, 2016, http://www.regnumchristi.org/english/articulos/articulo.phtml?se=363andca=341andte=876andid=34476

3. Fernández-Carvajal, *In Conversation with God*, vol. 2, 314.

4. Linda ZagZebski, "Virtue Ethics | Moral Virtues | Loyalty," YouTube video, August 28, 2015, https://www.youtube.com/watch?v=kKwPUkSCNDg.

5. Sadlier Religion, "Catholic Virtues Series: Loyal Loved Ones," *We Believe and Share* (blog), September 3, 2014, accessed October 10, 2016, http://www.sadlier.com/religion/we-believe-and-share/bid/102911/Catholic-Virtues-Series-Loyal-Loved-Ones.

6. Jenn Johns, "8 Types of Gossip, 26 Bible Verses," *Going by Faith* (blog), May 2, 2012, http://goingbyfaith.com/types-of-gossip.

7. Giving Generosity

1. Mike Campbell, "Katherine," *Behind the Name*, accessed October 29, 2016, http://www.behindthename.com/name/katherine.

2. Raymond Capua, *The Life of St. Catherine of Siena*, trans. George Lamb (Charlotte, NC: Tan Books, 2003), 10.

3. Ibid., 103–104.

4. Ibid., 304.

5. John Paul II, Address of John Paul II to the Young People in Auckland, New Zealand, November 22, 1986, http://w2.vatican.va/content/john-paul-ii/en/speeches/1986/november/documents/hf_jp-ii_spe_19861122_giovani-auckland-nuova-zelanda.html.

6. Catherine of Siena, *Catherine of Siena—Passion for the Truth, Compassion for Humanity: Selected Spiritual Writings,* ed. Mary O'Driscoll (New Rochelle, NY: New City Press, 1993), 76.

7. Emily J. Cook, "Hospitality Is Biblical—and It's Not Optional," CatholicCulture.org, February 2006, accessed October 29, 2016, https://www.catholicculture.org/culture/library/view.cfm?recnum=6981.

8. Catherine of Siena, *Catherine of Siena,* 71.

8. Pondering Prayerfulness

1. Augustine, *The Confessions of St. Augustine,* trans. by John K. Ryan (New York: Image Books, 1960), 1.1.43.

2. "Ephrem the Syrian Quotes," accessed October 16, 2016, http://www.azquotes.com/author/25105-Ephrem_the_Syrian.

3. Capua, *The Life of St. Catherine of Siena,* 302.

4. John Paul II, "The Visitation Is the Prelude to Jesus' Mission," accessed October 10, 2016, http://www.passionistnuns.org/Saints/StElizabethVisitation/index.htm.

5. Edward P. Sri, *Walking with Mary: A Biblical Journey* (New York: Crown Publishing Group, 2013), 70, Kindle edition.

6. Denise Bossert, *Gifts of the Visitation: Nine Spiritual Encounters with Mary and Elizabeth* (Notre Dame, IN: Ave Maria Press, 2015), 65.

7. Rhonda De Sola Chervin, ed., *Quotable Saints* (Oak Lawn, IL: CMJ Marian Publishers, 2003) 127.

Michele Faehnle is a contributor to *CatholicMom.com*, codirector of the Columbus Catholic Women's Conference, and coauthor of *Divine Mercy for Moms*. She earned a bachelor of science degree (cum laude) in nursing from Franciscan University of Steubenville in 1999. After twelve years as a labor and delivery nurse, she left nursing to be home with her growing family and answer the call to the New Evangelization. Faehnle has spoken at the National Shrine of Divine Mercy and to several women's groups and conferences, including 1:38 Women, Mothering with Grace Annual Mothers' Conference, Indiana Catholic Women's Conference, and the online Catholic Conference for Moms. Faehnle has appeared on EWTN's *At Home with Jim and Joy* and a number of Catholic radio programs. She and her husband, Matthew, have four children and live in Columbus, Ohio.

Emily Jaminet is a contributor to *CatholicMom.com* and coauthor of *Divine Mercy for Moms*. She serves on the leadership team of the Columbus Catholic Women's Conference. Jaminet earned a bachelor's degree in mental health and human services from Franciscan University of Steubenville in 1998. After several years working at the Pittsburgh Leadership Foundation, Jaminet moved back to Columbus, Ohio, to be a stay-at-home mom.

Jaminet offers a daily segment called *A Mother's Moment* on St. Gabriel Catholic Radio and Mater Dei Radio. She has spoken to several women's groups and conferences, including 1:38 Women, Mothering with Grace Annual Mothers' Conference, Indiana Catholic Women's Conference, Women's Day of Reflection for Homeschoolers, and the online Catholic Conference for Moms. Jaminet has appeared on EWTN's *At Home with Jim and Joy* and a number of Catholic radio programs. She and her husband, John, have seven children and live in Columbus, Ohio.

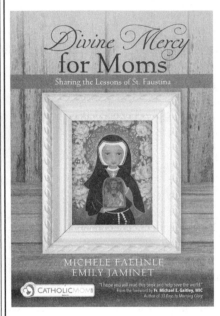